MW00694755

THE SECRET TO KNOWING YOURSELF

MY MEDITATION JOURNEY

KELLY M PACHECO

ISBN: 978-7331419-0-1

Library of Congress Control Number: 2020910597

Copyright © 2020 by Kelly M Pacheco

All rights reserved.

No part of this book may be reproduced in any form or by any electronic or mechanical means, including information storage and retrieval systems, without written permission from the author, except for the use of brief quotations in a book review.

NOTE FROM THE AUTHOR

This book is like no other published so far. To be able to understand it and absorb its magic, you will need to bear in mind that it was initially written to prove whether the practice of a meditation technique called Kriya Yoga could guarantee spiritual enlightenment.

In the first pages, you will see how anxious to prove the effectiveness of this method; I devoted myself faithfully to the daily practice of that ancient technique. Those early pages also have the dazzling power to take you by the hand, allowing you to travel with me, and experience how a new and fascinating world opens up before your eyes.

It is not until you are halfway through this book that the story evolves into something else entirely. At this turning point, when the effectiveness of the meditation technique is demonstrated, the pages begin to reveal how this path to enlightenment is, in fact, the secret to knowing oneself and how that enlightenment also represents the spark that is lit within us, allowing us to see our Higher Self.

Immediately after I discovered that enlightenment is nothing else but the knowledge, awareness, and understanding of ourselves, I could have rewritten the book only addressing the issue of how to get to know ourselves. However, if I had done so, I would have written one of those millions of self-help books already published on that subject, still standing on bookshelves waiting to be read.

Unlike others, this book does not claim to be the bearer of the absolute truth, nor does it try to force you to follow specific steps; on the contrary, it was written hoping to awaken within you the inspiration to find your own path, and your own answers. Thus, I ask you not to feel disappointed or lost when you don't find in these pages exercises or steps to follow. Instead, be attentive, because this book, like many of the magic books out there, has a specific message for each person and must be read with your heart wide open.

Magic is always invisible to our eyes and minds, which is why, instead of reading and analyzing the formal content of this work, I invite you to read and perceive how my words and experiences make you feel. I encourage you to notice what they awaken within you and, most importantly, what they inspire you to do because inspiration, as I was able to discover, is one of those mysterious forces of the Universe that holds the key to materialization.

INTRODUCTION

The thought that changed everything

Today is September 1, 2018. I am in Playa Langosta, Costa Rica, completing the entire outline of this book. I cannot envision an introduction without sharing with you the thought that started the ripple effect that materialized this book in your hands, allowing you to read the experiences and realizations of the past two years of my life, as I followed the path towards spiritual enlightenment.

The thought that triggered the domino effect that shook my entire life appeared in my mind more than a year ago, while reading the book *Autobiography of a Yogi* by Paramahansa Yogananda. Within this magical book, there is a section where its author explains how Kriya Yoga is a "scientific method" used to achieve enlightenment.

As soon as I read this assertion, I had to pause and look away from the book, in order to assimilate what my eyes had just read. That phrase repeated over and over in my troubled mind: "a scientific method to achieve spiritual enlightenment." I felt that someone was playing a joke on me.

I had not read those two words together—scientific method—since high school and, for sure, I had never linked them to spirituality. If that phrase contained any truth, then that right there was my Holy Grail, the treasure that I had been seeking for most of my adult life.

I looked away from the book again to double-check that I wasn't dreaming, and as I looked around, everything seemed even more unreal. I was surrounded by a cloudless sky with a luscious mélange of blues that met someplace in the distance with a vast ocean. I saw waves unleashing their fury and splashing white against the black rock formations of a cliff, where dozens of seals rested, unaffected. The uninhabited surrounding mountains seemed to be the other witnesses of that moment, at the same time confirming the solitude and rawness of that place.

It wasn't until I suddenly heard voices around me that I realized I was in a car with my family. After a few seconds of recollection, everything came back to me: we were on vacation traversing California's Big Sur. We had left a small town that morning, making our way through the park towards San Francisco.

During those minutes of connection with reality, my mind had already circumvented the shock and developed the thought that changed everything: *If someone had dared to claim that there was a proven method to achieve spiritual enlightenment, I could not do anything else but try it.*

While watching through the window, lost in that thought, and totally mired in a deep state of happiness, I was brought back to reality by the commotion inside the car, where everyone was praising the beauty and taking pictures of the place. I could not concentrate on what they were saying as I was still floating in a state of bliss that I could not share; none of the people in the car could ever understand the magnitude of the gift this book and this moment had given to me.

I didn't even want to continue reading; something within me assured me that I had already found what I was looking for. And it was all contained in those lines. This present was so precious that I was going to wait for the solitude of another perfect moment to continue reading the map to my treasure. I closed the book and looked around, while a smile of complicity with the Universe escaped from my lips. And for the rest of our drive through the Big Sur, I remained motionless in the back seat, delighted by the landscape extravaganza and the significance of the moment.

How everything changed

Those moments lived on, those breaths taken, and those words flying through my head catalyzed the sequence of events that introduced me to the most accessible and simple practice that has since changed my life. You see, at that time, to reach a higher consciousness or enlightenment meant everything to me. It meant arriving where we all needed and wanted to be.

At that time, I was so shy and so humble with my desires that I would have been thrilled to find a path to follow. Kriya Yoga not only showed it to me, it also illuminated my way through it, dissipating all of my fears and allowing me to see all the magic along the way.

Thanks to this path, I have received the most beautiful and treasured gifts that I could have ever dreamed of. From time to time, when I least expect it, I get tiny sips of the enlightenment I was yearning for, and because of those few tiny sips, everything I have lived through until now has been worth it!

I have no urge to reach enlightenment. This here and this now is so enticing that the future and the past have finally lost their power over me since they cannot offer anything this real, this intense.

When I look closely at all the transformations that I have experienced through this path, there is one that is very close to my heart, and that still manages to keep me in awe every day. Somehow, after several months of continuous meditation practice, I realized that I was able to connect with a Divine Knowledge that exists within me. This knowledge doesn't come from the books that I read, people that I talk to, or any gurus. It comes only from the depths of my being.

In those magical moments, when this connection appears and I come into contact with this divinity, I can hear it whispering the answers to some of the existential questions that always haunted me, allowing me to develop "my" new understanding and perception of life.

Today, my eyes witness an entirely new world, my mind perceives everything differently, and my life is felt on much deeper levels. For the first time, I am aware of my consciousness—a faculty that I often heard about, but never truly understood. This awareness has helped me to establish very strong bonds with myself, my body, nature, and the Universe. All these internal changes and connections have attracted experiences that I had never been exposed to before—and I certainly don't mean anything supernatural like levitating or teleporting. These are intimate and sublime experiences, produced within me by simply existing, being, and breathing.

As you progress through this reading, you will notice how this path has secretly guided me to discover my Highest Purpose in life. Dredging up from the depths of my being, a dream that had been buried since I was a child and that today materializes, filling every day of my life with an inexhaustible ecstasy and inspiration.

Following this path became my priority. For me, it was not only important to follow the method and achieve the result; no, for me, it was much more significant than that. Yogananda was bold enough to affirm that Kriya Yoga was a scientific method, which means that every time it is used, it will yield the same results: spiritual enlightenment. Therefore, I needed to have proof of the whole process, to understand how it works, and how any change occurs. At the same time, I set out to be impartial enough to recognize its faults. This would be the greatest present I could ever give to myself.

At those early stages, the idea of a book was never on my mind; at that time, the world only revolved around me. The idea of writing a book only arrived after a few months of practicing Kriya Yoga, when the changes in me were so profound that they led me to believe that the scientific method was working.

Only when the world stopped revolving around me did I begin to fantasize about a book where I could share my story, helping others to embark on their journey and multiply all the magic I felt when reading *Autobiography of a Yogi*.

Since the beginning, this has been a solo trip. It has always been just me, my meditation, my diary, my self-study, my yoga (asanas), and my reading. This book contains exactly that: the first twelve months of that wonderful path, the whole process, and some of the lines written in my diary during those days.

What I was given by *Autobiography of a Yogi* and by those 365 days has been something I could never have imagined. Many people talk about God, the Divine, or a Higher Power. However, words are just words, they form an opinion, and with that, you could never convince a skeptic, as they cannot be seen, felt, or experienced.

The practice of Kriya Yoga has given me the opportunity to experience that God, that Divine, that Higher Power or whatever you wish to call it. Every time I find myself in contact with it, it expands my consciousness to new heights, giving me the certainty that it has always been and will always be here within me.

If you ask me whether I am fully enlightened, I will tell you that I'm not. I can say that I am more enlightened than yesterday, but not completely. I might also say that I feel with every piece of my being that I'm definitely on the path to a higher consciousness. I have tasted small sips of it! And it's much better than any drug! Those sips take me to the highest states of being, without the need for alcohol, drugs, or brainwashing.

This ecstasy comes from feeling with my whole being the connection with the Universe, so I am simply there: high on reality, high on my connection with nature, and high on my own existence. My mind is always there, alert, aware at every second of what is happening but still in the back seat. So I become like the trees that allow the breeze to move its branches and foliage, like the sea waves, becoming the foam that caresses the sand. This is definitely the wildest trip I have ever experienced.

Before that day in Big Sur, I had seen magic appear in my life only twice, but after that day, I started to see magic all the time, and everywhere. Synchronicities and events that seemed like gifts specially destined for me suddenly materialized in my life. So, how could I be wrong if I was walking on a path that provided me with so much magic?

I was raised in a man-made world, and as I grew up, the ties that bound me to that world had grown strong. Gradually and over time, I began to feel those ties as nasty roots that kept me tied to a repulsive world that I no longer wanted to be a part of. However, when all the magic of this path began to appear, those roots started to lose control over me; then, in a last attempt to hold me back, they clung harder to claim their sovereignty, but my eyes were already open. I had already experienced who I really was, and I realized that I was all things: beauty, freedom, magic, sweetness, and flow.

For the first time in my life, I was certain that those roots were not part of me, as I was once led to believe. The only thing left to do at that time was to let myself be stripped from them, and from that moment on, be my pure Self—free, beautiful, magical, sweet, and detached.

Before I begin to lose my most skeptical readers with my floating experiences and all the magic I see thanks to this path, I will share with you some of the measurable changes I have experienced thanks to Kriya Yoga. If you wonder how these changes occurred, I have summarized my version of how meditation works in the Afterword at the end of the book.

In the past, I lived with a daily stress level of 90 to 99 percent every day and was fully present about 10 percent of the time. Today, my stress level is between 5 and 10 percent, depending on the day, and I am fully present between 70 and 80 percent of the time.

Before, my mind worked continuously to anticipate how everything could go wrong. Today my mind continues to be sharp but is only used when necessary.

To be totally honest, at the beginning of the road, there was only practice, practice, and more practice. Nothing could assure me that every day I sat down to meditate was contributing to any change. Although small changes began to appear after a couple of months, the ones that could be really accounted for started happening seven months after I began my Kriya Yoga practice. Frankly, there is nothing more to it than just sitting for an hour or two a day to meditate.

Many people profit from our spiritual quest and use the words "yoga" and "meditation" as they please. Running away from all of that, I decided to follow no one, and I realized that the more I meditated, the less I needed guidance. Gradually, I began to become my own guru, and the only words that came out of my mouth during difficult times were "keep on practicing," and that was precisely what I needed to hear because, when I continued, more magic appeared.

We are so powerful, so capable of accomplishing anything. We only need to realize that we are the creators of our awakening path and our reality. We do not have to follow others; we only need to have the courage to travel inwards, without maps or guides, to reach the place within where all the treasures await.

Be bold enough to travel alone, to not listen to anyone but yourself.

1

THE BIRTH OF THIS BOOK

FROM MY FIRST steps on this path, I took it very seriously, almost like a full-time job. I needed to make sure that I followed everything this practice entailed. I also wanted to have some sort of evidence that could serve as proof of what happened inwardly while I strictly followed this method.

That's how I committed myself to one hour of meditation and another hour to sit down and journal about my experiences, translating into words everything that happened within and around me during this entire journey.

Those lines became my life, my mirror, my judge, and my release; somehow they became fingerprints of my everyday existence. In that journal, I could be truthful with myself in ways that I had never been before. I never read previous entries. I was always so happy to write and confess in it that yesterday's pages were never as relevant as the ones I was working on. Many times, I wondered if those lines revealed a change in me, but I was so fascinated with everything that was boiling inside me that I wanted to wait until I had been following the path for a full year to read them.

As time went by and the practice continued, I began to feel the sweetest, most peaceful, and dazzling experiences of being. They were simply too beautiful and too profound to keep them hidden on those pages. Thus, I was overcome with a fervent desire to share everything I was experiencing with anyone who was willing to listen.

All I could think about in those days was: How did nobody tell me that something like this could be experienced? How come nobody talks about this? How are there not hundreds of books that talk about it? But in reality there were thousands upon thousands of books and millions upon millions of people talking about the subject. It was me who had absolutely ignored all of it with thousands of excuses. I remember that I used to believe that it was impossible for someone like me to experience any kind of magic. I also believed that I would never be able to leave my mind blank for more than two seconds. Sometimes, it was easier for me to believe that many of those people were making up their stories, since none of them could really explain what was happening while they were meditating.

I remember that my need for knowledge about enlightenment began many years ago. In those days, I was looking for a book written by someone who was as mundane as me, someone who shared their journey and could explain the enlightenment process based on their own experience. I was intrigued to know how to find the right path, and what was achieved by walking it. I guess in those days I wanted to at least believe that it was feasible, but even though I did my best, I was never able to find that book I was looking for.

Only after seeing everything I had achieved in such a short time through the practice of Kriya Yoga did I decide to write that very book that I would have loved to read for years, a book where I would share my path, the good and the bad. For me, the most important thing was not reaching the destination, but all the experiences lived along the way. That was how this book was conceived.

Throughout this journey, I have been able to share my story with those closest to me, and they have been inspired by it. One of the most precious moments for me is when someone can see or experience magic for the first time. I can see the exact moment when their innermost being witnesses the sparkle of their Highest Self.

After that moment, nothing is the same; they have now caught a glimpse of greatness, and can recognize that there is something more—here, there, everywhere. After that day, they are hooked. Their quest has begun, and with it, everything that was in darkness begins to light up.

My intention is not that you follow my steps. The sole purpose of this book is to show you that it is possible for all of us to discover our true Self and walk on the path towards enlightenment or Divine Knowledge. This truly is an outstanding and mesmerizing journey, with indescribable experiences that have led me to exist on another level and to live a different life altogether.

I chose the Kriya Yoga method because I felt a connection with it that I couldn't ignore; every word I read about it resonated within me at such a high level that I could instantly feel it as true. If you would ask me, I would tell you that I believe that Kriya Yoga is not the only method to achieve enlightenment or to connect you with a Higher Consciousness. I am sure there are many others. I have only practiced this scientific method, but after more than two years of daily meditation, I can demonstrate thanks to this book how this practice guides us towards a Higher Consciousness. I can't confirm that it will help you reach enlightenment, because I have not achieved it myself, but I am absolutely sure that I am on the right path to it.

Turning my diaries and self-study pages into a book has not been an easy task. At first, those pages were filled with beautiful accounts of experiences in which I felt myself floating while meditating or in which I was immersed in a sublime state of absolute bliss. But, at some point along the way, those pages metamorphosed, and as a result, they let me see profound changes within me. Some of those changes were easy to track through the pages, but there were others that had left no trace in my journals; yet they still had happened, they were real, and they were now part of me, part of the new person I had become.

On the other hand, there was also an obvious difference in writing. Initially I was completely self-centered, a selfish person, focused only on me, my problems, and their possible solutions. Little by little, page by page, my transformation into a new person was evident; by the end of the journal I no longer spoke about my mundane life or my problems. Instead, I explored my new perception of life. Suddenly, according to those pages, I had built some pillars that were now fundamental to me. I wrote pages and pages about my relationship with nature and with everything around me, and although the mundane was less mentioned, I could read between the lines that it was still present.

The Best Advice in This Book

For those of you who are like my sister and want to know the entire contents of a book in the first few pages, I'll give you that treat. In the following paragraphs, I will share with you a story that carries the essence of this book, illustrating how we only need a second for our lives to change. The story portrays how doors within us open into parallel worlds, and if we are courageous enough to believe in them, we will immediately be granted access. I invite you to read it carefully.

What if I invite you to take my hand and go back in time to the era of the caveman? While there, we can take a look at their simple lives, see how they lived primarily led by their instincts. We will be able to see their caves, see them hunt animals when they are hungry, see their vulnerability to the weather, among many other things. Imagine now that while we are there, you tell these men the following:

"There is something inside your head called a brain, and if you connect with it, use it, and develop it, eventually you will have everything you could dream of and much more. You could fly through the skies, stop physical pain with a little white stone, have a strange-looking box in your house, filled with food, without going hunting, and millions of other incredible possibilities like these."

What do you think will happen next? Well, of course, these cavemen will eat you and all your nonsense in a second.

So, now I want you to imagine that I approach you and whisper in your ear:

"Within you there is a force of unimaginable power called Divine Energy, and if you connect with it and use it, in time, you will have everything you could dream of and much more. You could fill your days with hours of an inexhaustible ecstasy called inspiration, you wouldn't have to look for love outside yourself, as love would calmly lay within you, life would be a luscious adventure that you would have never even dared to dream and millions of other incredible possibilities like these."

What do you think will happen next? Would you eat me alive or would you try to connect with that Divine Energy?

We have been on the same path for centuries and centuries, looking for a God that will give us the answers to our questions or following others who made us believe they have them. But no, the answers are not in the skies or in books, much less in others. All the answers are within us.

We have been led to believe that we are the way we dress, the lifestyle we follow, the professions we exercise, the activities we like, and all the labels we have identified ourselves with throughout our lives. But in reality, we are none of those banal and mundane descriptions. When I decided to title this work *The Secret to Knowing Yourself*, I wasn't referring to that superficial level to which we are all accustomed, I was referring to what is underneath it all, to the source of everything, to what some people call spirit or soul and I refer through this book as Self, Divine Energy, and Divine Knowledge.

Meditation, and specifically Kriya Yoga, is that secret passage that leads us not only to recognize that we are that Divine Energy but to experience it with every atom of our body and interpret it with every faculty of our mind.

The only effort required of us is to believe that it is possible, and I am not talking about blindly believing—not at all. At first, believing that there is a tiny possibility that all the answers are within us will be more than enough. From then on, we only need to take the time to look inward, to quiet our minds, and listen carefully to what is meant for us to hear. Then, and only then, we can connect with our Higher Self and that Divine Knowledge that is within us and with everything that makes up this Universe.

When you are looking for mundane answers or mundane things, you can easily use mundane methods. When you want a new car, you can try to make more money to buy it. But when we want things that go beyond the mundane, when we are looking for intangible assets like happiness, peace, bliss, and a Higher Consciousness, we need to step it up, and not just a notch, I mean wildly and exponentially, because none of those mundane methods will work.

You cannot work harder to be peaceful and happy. No book on *10 Ten Steps to a Higher Consciousness* or *How to Be Blissful in 10 Ten Days* will help you. No, they won't cut it.

You need to do things that are out of the ordinary, a bit more magical and intangible, to achieve out of the ordinary, magic, and intangible results—and for me, those practices are meditation and Kriya Yoga.

2

THE "ME" BEFORE AND THE "ME" AFTER

The "Me" Before

JUST TWO YEARS AGO, I was one of the worst human beings that existed, and if you ask my ex-husband, he will definitely agree with that. I was selfish, obnoxious, unbearable, controlling, a liar, unfaithful, jealous, and envious. I smoked cigarettes non-stop, and marijuana sporadically. I drank alcohol as a hobby. I used people and let others use me. Believing blindly that I was the center of the Universe had led me to hurt people whom I deeply loved. So yes, I was one of the worst people alive.

If in those days you had asked me what I believed in, I would have told you that I did believe that there was something bigger than us, but I had not yet found what it was, and I was actively looking for it.

My Belief System

My skepticism began at an early age. You see, I was raised in the Catholic religion, but by the age of ten, I had already broken most of the Ten Commandments. My mother, who was also a

Catholic although she never went to church, somehow forced me to do my First Communion.

During what is called Catechism studies, I discovered how deep in hell I was. Every book I read made me believe that I was a terrible person, a sinner, but the most disturbing was that I really felt that I was a good kid. Yes, I lied frequently and I was more curious and active than the rest, but I was still good.

Everything I had done until that point wasn't done with bad intention, but rather out of curiosity, boredom, or even copying what I saw around me. At that age, I had no idea that other kids behaved in similar ways. In my mind, I was a terrible kid, a sinner.

The more I studied, the more I thought there was no way out. No regret, no confession could prevent me from ending in hell. The rigor of all the nuns and priests at the church I attended never allowed me to believe that after the Sacrament of Penance, I could be absolved of all my sins.

Anyway, my Catholicism was short-lived, as the days prior to my First Communion ended up being the last days for me on that path. I still remember clearly the day I took the Sacrament of Penance, as it became the worst day of my childhood and caused the most extreme moments of turbulence in my heart.

It was a Saturday morning; my messy hair told a story of a long sleepless night. At the church, more than one hundred children were sitting in the pews waiting for their turn, and of course, I was seated in the front row, being one of the first to confess.

When the moment arrived for me to enter the room where the confession was going to take place, I realized that not only was I sweating, but my whole body was shaking. As soon as I entered, I noticed that the sacrament was not going to take place in one of the standard confessional boxes. In fact, I had to do the Sacrament of Penance sitting on a chair in front of the priest, facing him, while all the nuns ran from side to side as if they had a million things to do.

Once I was seated in front of the priest, my heart started to gallop with such intensity that it prevented any words from escaping my lips. After a few seconds of struggling internally to calm myself down, I realized how futile that effort was. The priest was already looking at me impatiently. Finally, I felt something wanted to come out of my mouth, something that might put an end to that torture, something that could explain everything that was happening in my head. Instead, the only words that managed to escape from my lips formed the desperate sentence, "I am a bad person!"

As soon as those words were pronounced and I realized their meaning, tears began to come out desperately from my eyes. I remember trying to cover my face with my little hands to stop and hide them, but it was impossible. They kept pouring down as if they had been locked inside me for a long time.

The commotion took a tremendous toll on me. I knew there was no going back from that. I looked around; and the nuns were perplexed with their eyes fixed on me. I guess nobody knew what to do, and I couldn't do anything other than get up from the chair and run away. I left that little room next to the altar in no time. Everybody was speechless. I continued running desperately through the nave, passing by all the kids waiting for their turn, with their eyes set on me. Once outside, I didn't know what to do, so I kept running farther and farther.

Looking back, I can recognize that event as the first time that my heart was shattered into pieces by the mundane world. It was the first time in my life that I was led to believe that what I felt inward was not real, that the only thing that was real was the set of black-and-white rules that governed the mundane world.

At that time, it didn't matter that I could feel my innocence, my open heart, or my loving spirit. The only thing that mattered was outside of me, and it was based on the way people perceived me, my actions, and their results.

It is almost impossible for me to remember what happened next. What I do know is that my mom still forced me to do the First Communion. However, when the day arrived, I wasn't angry or sad; on the contrary, I was happy, because I could feel and smell that my freedom was near. I knew that after that day no one would ever again force me to set foot in a church.

From that day on, I began to live my life believing in God but not in religion. My communication with my God was direct— there were no rules to follow or churches to visit. A small statuette of the baby Jesus became the image of my God, and I didn't need to pray, I only talked with my little God when I felt it was necessary. My only commandment was to feel in my heart that I was good, and in those years, I definitely was, until time and adulthood moved me away from that God, and I simply stopped believing.

Today I can say that when I stopped believing in God, it was not the happiest period of my life. Ironically, while thinking that I was a free spirit, the opposite was happening within me. That atheist lifestyle brought an unbearable burden on me. You see... losing the faith that God will always be by your side to help you, to take care of you, and to guide you leaves you alone against the world. Suddenly, I became the only one responsible for everything that happened to me—no one could protect me or help me. So, slowly over time, that superhuman responsibility began to develop within me a frantic need to control everything: not only what was related to me, but also everything that was happening around me.

All of this gradually took me to a state where I was emotionally and physically tense most of the time. Of course, I was unable to notice that tension since it had been growing slowly inward since I started my adult life. As time went by, the need to control everything began to take over my life altogether. I wanted people close to me to do exactly what I wanted and I only had friends I could manipulate or who behaved in a way that was acceptable to me.

Because of this, all my relationships began to crack. My whole family was afraid of me. I dictated everything that needed to be done and how it should be done. This situation not only destroyed my relationships, but it was also destroying my body, as all my muscles and organs lived in a continuous straining; even while I slept my eyes were so tightly closed that I seemed like I was having constant nightmares. This tension had accompanied me for so many years that it was impossible for me to loosen up. Sadly, my body had completely forgotten how to relax.

I knew that my skepticism and the denial of a Higher Power had pushed me into being a "control freak," and that was a life not well lived. At that time, I was torn: I wanted to believe that a Higher Power existed, but my rejection of any kind of religion and the fear of being brainwashed by any other form of spiritualism was so strong that it felt impossible to find a way forward.

That state of dissatisfaction took me to many places in search of answers. Until a day when I attended the event of one of the most famous motivational speakers in the United States. There while practicing an intense guided meditation, I was able to experience and feel for the first time in my life that Higher Power and the state of absolute happiness that surrounds it.

What was incredibly strange was that I had not attended this event looking for something spiritual; who goes to those kinds of events looking for that? I went there strictly for the mundane; to be more specific, I went there looking to find a way to earn more money, and in those days that speaker was the guy.

The event took place in December 2014. I remember it clearly because that year my life had changed dramatically. I was thirty-five years old, and I had just bought the first house that felt like a home. I had separated from my husband, and while finalizing the divorce proceedings, I had moved in with my son, Troy, who at that time was four years old. It had taken me two years to get out of that marriage, and during that time I had a low-paying job as a property manager that allowed me to learn how to make money with real estate and to save enough to maintain my independence.

In those days my only interest, besides trying to control everything around me, was to produce as much money as possible. If you think about it, for a control freak to make more money, it is synonymous with more power.

Money gave me a false sense of relief, making me believe that if I had more of it, I would be safer and thus able to relax. The reality was that money had become my religion, the only thing I believed in, and the only thing that I couldn't get enough of. It was the first thing I thought about when I woke up and my last thought before going to bed at night.

The event consisted of four days in which you try to discover how to take your life to the "next level." More than five thousand people were attending. I didn't really know what to expect, but I never would have imagined something like what I experienced in those four days.

The moment the doors of the gigantic conference hall at the Waldorf Astoria in Boca Raton opened, madness took place. All the attendees and organizers began shouting, jumping, and dancing, while songs by Rihanna and similar artists played loudly from every speaker.

Everybody was so pumped that it seemed that they had been there before, like they already knew the drill. And in fact, most of them had. People were running, screaming, and talking to each other, filled with a sudden euphoria. It was evident that it was my first time. I was not screaming, I was not singing, I was not jumping on the floors or on top of the chairs. I was just shamelessly looking around, trying to figure out what could cause five thousand people to act like that. Was it something in the water? Was this a modern version of a cult?

It took me the whole day to stop paying attention to what was happening around me and to concentrate on the actual presentation. Nevertheless, when I came back to the event the next day, I felt so out of place that I wanted to quit. I wanted to go home, to run away from all of those "freaks" and their "cult-like" event. Thankfully I didn't do it, because on that second day, the motivational speaker made me perceive something that didn't cost the five thousand dollars he charged for the event; it was worth every single penny in the world.

This gigantic man had been introduced to a meditation through an organization in India and had included it as part of the event because, as he mentioned, it had worked wonders on him and his wife. At the beginning, when he started talking about all the benefits of that miraculous practice, I didn't give it much importance because I was still thinking about the possibility that the whole event was a farce and wondering if I should have left. However, for some strange reason, when that man began to give the instructions, I found myself following them to the letter.

That unexpected meditation quickly took hold of me, plunging me into deep relaxation. After a few minutes in that state, I began to feel that something was going to happen; however, this anticipation never affected my deep relaxation. After a few more seconds, a tingling sensation began by seizing my fingers and then spreading rapidly through the rest of my body. In the blink of an eye, what had begun as a timid tingling sensation had totally taken over my body and suddenly evolved into intense currents of energy vibrating within me. I reached such a high state of alertness and consciousness that in the few seconds that followed, I became a multidimensional being.

I was fully aware of what was happening in my body, in my mind, around me, and in many other dimensions. All these sources were providing me with fragments of information every second. I would have imagined that I would be scared during such an unusual experience; however, I was calm, composed, and absorbing it all. I felt like I suddenly had all the superpowers, but I didn't know how to use them or what to do with them.

Immediately, I began to feel something like a warm hug. I could feel the warmth of the embrace, although there was no one around me. Nothing could bring me back at that moment. I was fully aware of the perplexity of my mind, but I was also expectant of what was going to happen next, and what happened next was something that shifted my whole existence.

Unexpectedly, I found myself immersed in a strange, immense, and absolute knowledge. Little by little, I realized that this knowledge was everywhere. The strangest thing was that I was floating in it, because my being was made of its essence, and while I was there floating in that knowledge and in that absolute bliss, I began to ask question after question and, surprisingly, all the answers were there for me.

After a few seconds, there were no more questions, none of that was important to me anymore. The bliss and the knowledge within me and around me were all that mattered, all I wanted to feel, and all I wanted to know. And in that instant I realized that this knowledge and this bliss were the essence of everything that existed.

While floating in that magical and ethereal world, I could feel how my mind was alert, trying to filter everything in order to assign a logical explanation to what was happening. Once my brain understood the impossibility of the task, it surrendered and decided to name God as the source of those unexplained and divine forces I was experiencing. As soon as my mind arrived at that conclusion, I was baffled. I couldn't understand how I, one of the worst people in the world and without a doubt one of the most skeptical, was being given the wild opportunity to experience God.

I couldn't help but go back to the exact day when I had stopped believing in God, and while I was visiting those old memories, tears poured out of my closed eyes. I was still in a trance, so I wasn't able to move to stop them, so they ran freely down my cheeks.

There I was, totally devoted to the experience, floating and floating until the moment arrived for all of it to depart. Once everything vanished, I was left feeling the aftermath of the most profound and elevated state I had ever experienced.

When it was time for me to open my eyes and reintegrate into this world, I felt no need to move so I stayed in the same chair seated for more than half an hour, while the people around me returned to their euphoria, jumping on top of the chairs and singing in unison. I was there, unaffected by all that madness, still in disbelief of what had just happened to me. How to explain that after almost ten years of not believing in any God or Higher Power, I received such a present?

That was my first experience with that Higher Power, and it was so intense that during the next three days, I was in a catatonic bliss state, just feeling, smiling, and floating. I didn't even want to move. Everything was so intensely felt, all of my senses were so aroused, that even food and sounds I had lived with all my life seemed new to me. Undoubtedly, for me the most dazzling after-effects were the immense waves of love pouring out of me for days and days.

Unfortunately, as the days went by, all those sensations began to fade, until they were finally gone. Weeks later, I tried desperately to connect with the Indian organization bestowing those blessings, but it was taken over by Westerners interested in monetizing that experience and had totally changed.

What I got from that encounter was the confirmation that a Higher Power existed. To be fully honest, when I had this experience, I had zero knowledge of other religions or spiritual practices. Those topics were the last ones in my conversations. I even remember arguing with my brother one day because I thought Buddhism was not a religion. The only thing that I knew was that I had been running away from Catholicism since I was ten years old, until my late twenties when I became an atheist.

However, after that experience, this needed to change. I had assigned the name of God to what I had experienced, but the reality was that I didn't feel comfortable with that designation. I felt as if I was missing several pieces of a puzzle. Deep down, I knew there was something else I couldn't identify with my limited knowledge; therefore, I decided to change the name of God for what I had really experienced, and that is how from that moment on, all my references of God changed to Higher Power, Higher Knowledge, or Higher Consciousness.

The transcendental episode sent me off on a quest through all of the spiritual practices that I could get in contact with, so I could experience it again. One day led to another until that day in Big Sur when I got Yogananda's book *Autobiography of a Yogi* in my hands and realized that I had found the door that had once closed on me. This time, I knew where the door was. I was magically given the key, and I could feel that those floating days that I had been longing for would come back to stay.

The "Me" after 365 Days of Kriya Yoga

I recognize that it is not easy for me to put into words what I feel now. I would love to make you feel the magic I feel and see the magic I see. I am living in this beautiful dream without being afraid of losing it because it depends only on me. I grew up believing that the idea of welcoming happiness without being afraid of its departure was a utopia, but it is not. That feeling is called absolute bliss, and it exists. I have tasted it.

Sometimes, that absolute bliss stays with me for the longest of times. It feels as if I'm in a bubble floating above everything else, and from there all I see is beauty. From inside my bubble everything moves in slow motion, the sun shines brighter, warming every particle of my being, and I am simply there, suspended in the air as the seconds pass. And yes, sometimes my bubble bursts and I fall back into the mundane, but I'm not afraid, because I know that my bubble still exists. I know it is real. I know that it has taken me to a higher level of consciousness, and I am certain that it will come back again when I least expect it, to lift me up and reward me with the same beauty again and again and again.

When I began to feel that absolute bliss, I wanted to feel it all the time. I became addicted to it, but over time, I learned to simply and gently surrender to it and let it come and go freely, like the waves of an ocean, while I remained motionless, profoundly moved by the power of its presence.

Other days I am granted an exquisite connection with everything; I walk outside my home and I get to feel in tune with the plants and the trees. I even feel the breeze in a different way. This connection makes me stop for a second to feel the sun caressing my body and the wind moving my hair. Where yesterday I only saw streets, cars, buildings, and people, today I only see nature: the sky, the trees, and the insects. Everything else is not essential to me and therefore nonexistent.

Only with time did I realize that this strong feeling for nature was only me recognizing that I am everything, that we are all the same and that we are all that nature. It is not just a "connection" or "being part" of nature. There are not humans, plants, and trees; on the contrary, we are all the plants, the trees, the sea, and the sky. We are all this perfection.

And I know that you will be reading and thinking that I have gone crazy, but if I am honest, nothing so radical would have ever crossed my mind until I got to experience it. In those moments, I feel that I simply exist and that I am destined, like all that nature, to follow the enigmatic flow of the Universe. During those minutes or hours, the sounds become more acute, the colors become more vibrant, the smells and flavors become more intense, and everything I touch is felt with my being, not with my mind.

In addition to the gifts of absolute bliss and the sensation of being "everything," this new consciousness has slowly washed away the tinted perception of life I grew up with. Today, my life is in a continuous flow, but I am not afraid of it anymore because I am no longer involved in the drama of fighting against the Universe. I live a life with less judgment towards situations and people, concentrating my energy on feeling and experiencing. Long ago seem the days in which I clung to everything. Today, I'm a child again, newly born into this new world, simply letting myself go while I look around in wonder.

My beliefs today are what I have chosen to believe. Kriya Yoga hasn't brainwashed me into believing in God or a Higher Self. I was just practicing by myself, and through practice, I noticed that my consciousness had new information and a new, broader perception of life. Today, I have a whole new belief system that came from a space within me, so it is part of me without being imposed by the world in which I live. These new beliefs are not engraved in stone either, as they change and evolve as I progress along this path.

At this point in my life, I don't believe in God or any specific religion. I have chosen to believe in what I felt during that event many years ago: a Divine Energy and a Divine Knowledge that possess all the answers of the Universe.

The way in which this Divinity operates is so mysterious that I don't waste my time trying to figure it out. The whys that once tormented me do not matter to me anymore as I no longer want to change or manipulate life. What I have found in this flow of life is pure perfection. Thus, I am just sitting here contemplating and enjoying every second of my existence.

3

HOW IT ALL BEGAN

To Receive What You Want, You Have to Ask for It

I REMEMBER the exact day on which I asked the Universe for the wishes that led me to the path that I follow so vehemently today, because they were invoked on the last day of 2016.

After reading the book entitled *The Secret* by Rhonda Byrne, my sister and I had started a little tradition where on the last day of every year we wrote down all of our wishes for the upcoming year.

Sometimes, I think back to those precious moments when I was writing those wishes, utterly oblivious to the marvelous life experiences coming ahead. To be totally honest, most of the items on my lists have always been material things, relatively easy to achieve. Usually, at the beginning of each year, those wishes became goals, which I worked hard to obtain.

The last days of 2016 were very special; together with my family we had visited several cities in Europe, and for our last stop we had rented a dream house located right in the heart of Amsterdam. I still remember the warm room I shared with my sister.

From our bedroom window, we could see the typical boats sailing along the narrow Nieuwe Herengracht Canal, celebrating early on the last day of the year.

It was a beautiful sunny day with a clear blue sky, the kind that wouldn't suggest at all that it was freezing outside. That afternoon I was lying on the bed with all the blankets I could find on top of me, looking through the window with that "last day of the year" feeling, in which the heart feels expectant for the year ahead and the mind is confused by a mixture of gratitude and melancholy for the year that passed. Yes, that dazzling sensation that anxiously waits for me every December, year after year with open arms and a cold bottle of champagne.

Once I finished writing my list, I noticed that it was very different from previous years. The items in it were no longer material things; on the contrary, they were experiences and feelings. I wanted to feel at peace and in harmony with everything around me, I wanted to work only two or three hours a day, and finally I wanted to find someone to settle down with as a family.

The content of that list had left me a little confused, so I paused, looked through the window, and imagined what my life would be like if all those wishes came true. In those seconds I realized that if everything I longed for materialized, my life would be totally different. Not only that, but I would also have to be a different person in order to experience all that. With that idea in mind, I shrugged my shoulders while saving the document, thinking that such a drastic change in me could only be achieved through some kind of hardcore, heavy magic.

These were not the kind of wishes I was used to, the ones where I could work on and measure the progress. I didn't have the slightest idea of how to achieve experiences and feelings. Although they couldn't be strategized or planned for success, something within me made me realize that if those wishes had come to me, it meant that there was at least a small chance that they would materialize, and that was all I needed.

That list had become a challenge for me, so I kept thinking, "We'll see," and with that last thought in my mind, I closed my laptop and began to prepare for the New Year's Eve celebrations.

The Magic Arrives and Love Appears

Six days before making that wish list in Amsterdam (the Universe seemed to have started planning everything as if it knew in advance what I was going to ask for), I had received a very short email saying: *"Merry Christmas, Kelly! I send you a big kiss, Joe."* I didn't reply to the email, and I wasn't planning to do it in the future.

Joe and I had a very turbulent relationship several years ago, and I say turbulent because of me. At that time, I was selfish, self-centered, and totally possessed by the mundane. I was in an insane pursuit of money. The more I had, the more I wanted, and the more I worked. In those days, I wanted all the wrong things and he didn't fit in any of them; on the contrary, he was very down to earth, kind, and hardworking—an honest man who enjoyed a simple life with his friends.

By that Christmas of 2016, I was so exhausted from dating the wrong guys that I felt I needed a long break from romantic relationships. The last person I got involved with was such a wrong fit that I remember the exact moment when I thought: *What am I doing?*

It was a gloomy day near the end of November, just a few weeks before that end of the year in Amsterdam. I was in Miami and had just arrived home when I received a call from the person I had been dating for a couple of months. He was in London, visiting his daughter. I remember telling him that I was returning from a children's party of one of my son's friends, to which he replied indifferently: "I'm not a kid's party kind of guy."

For me, that was a terrible impasse that I felt impossible to overcome, because I sincerely loved children's parties, even more so than adult parties. In fact, most of my afternoons revolve around my son, Troy, and his friends.

It was obvious that I had to get out of that relationship, but I still had my doubts. How could I doubt? It was obvious that this person was not a family type of guy. For a few seconds, I kept quiet and then I went over that last thought. A family guy? It had never even crossed my mind that I was looking for a family guy!

At that moment, I tried to quickly remember the wish lists I had written in previous years and all I could remember about them was: handsome, good body, good person, motivated, and successful, but "settle down" or "family man"? Those words were nowhere to be found. Why, if it was something I wanted, did I seem to have no idea about it? Why wasn't it part of my wishes?

Gradually, I began to establish the connections between the wish lists I had written and the kinds of people I had dated during those years, only to confirm that they were the exact replica of what I was asking for. Those wishes were as superficial and frivolous as the characters I stumbled upon.

At this point, I was so confused that it took me several days to process what was going on within me. Finally, I came to the conclusion that I had always wanted a person with whom to settle down, but somehow my frivolous and superficial mind wanted a man aligned with this frivolous person I had become.

This realization took me totally by surprise. I had learned, on the same day, that I wanted a man with whom to settle down and, as if that wasn't enough, I also realized that I was not the professional and driven woman I had convinced myself I was, but instead I was as frivolous and superficial as my wish lists.

Fortunately, that person never came back from London—or if he came, he never called—disappearing into thin air, which, given my situation, was the best thing that could have happened to me. Although I can't deny that my ego felt a bit bruised, the bewilderment I was experiencing from the revelations about myself overshadowed any other feelings that wanted to emerge.

I knew I needed a lot of time alone to process it all. December was fast approaching, and the idea ofspending the last weeks of the year in Europe sounded auspicious for new winds to blow different ideas my way.

Today, looking back on those years of my life, I can clearly see how lost I was. I had always attracted the wrong men to my life because I had no idea who I was or what I really wanted.

My life was a disaster because my mind was running it. I was totally disconnected from my "self" and that was also reflected in my working life, where I had practiced more than ten different professions in the last ten years and was unhappy in literally all of them. What a waste of time! I really don't know how I thought that winging it through life was going to actually work.

I must admit there were many occasions during those last ten years in which I sat down to think and try to find out what I really wanted from my relationships, from work, and from life in general. In those days I tried to discover my strengths and weaknesses as if they were clues that would lead me to find those answers at some point.

I wasted so many hours that led me in such different directions. If only I had noticed that everything I had been doing all those years I was doing on a mental level. Maybe, I would have realized that I was asking my mind what to do with my life without being aware that the mind doesn't want anything. The mind is only an instrument whose only job is to carry out tasks and obtain results, exactly like a computer that, no matter how fast or advanced, is totally incapable of wanting anything. The reality was that I didn't have to ask my mind what I wanted; that question would have to be asked to my own Self, to that operator that lives within me, that is within all of us.

If I am totally honest, I must admit that I was not looking for a man to settle down with because I was afraid to give me another chance. I had put myself in the wrong position in my last marriage and consequently those years turned out to be the most terrible and difficult ones of my life.

However, while holding up the phone to my ear talking to this person who was miles away on a cold and rainy winter night in London, I decided to accept that I really wanted to settle down with a man again, and that is how that idea ended up being carefully written as one of the wishes at the end of that year in Amsterdam. And as you will see, it was a realization that took almost no time to materialize.

We returned from Amsterdam the first week of January. I was so busy with work that I didn't have time for anything else. At the end of the month, my sister sent me an email with a video and a brief message that said: *"The guy in the video looks a lot like Joe."* As soon as I saw it, I remembered that I hadn't replied to his email.

My professional and personal lives were a disaster at that time. But I had found Joe flashing back into my life twice already: first, with his email and then, with my sister's message. I saw all of that as a sign I couldn't ignore, so I responded.

Joe called me as soon as he read my email. We had dinner a couple of times in the following weeks. I always missed our long conversations, accompanied by bottles of wine under the peaceful Miami sky. Since the first time I had seen him, I had always felt that he could be the right one for me, but I didn't give him a fair opportunity at that time.

What if everything that happened between us in the past remained in the past and we could start over? Would I be able to give that relationship a fair chance? What if he was the love of my life and I let him go? This time, I decided to forget all my preconceived ideas, not only about him, but also about myself, and give me the opportunity to discover him while discovering myself.

The next day was February 13, 2017. I heard someone knocking on my door and when I opened it, there he was with a huge bouquet of roses, wondering if I had someone to celebrate Valentine's Day with. We had already met about four times in the last two weeks, but we had never talked about something serious.

That night I decided to follow my own advice about not thinking. I took the roses with one hand and with the other I clung to his neck, stood on tiptoes, and said: "Yes... you!" and we kissed.

After that day, we couldn't stay away from each other. Two months later, he proposed. Soon after, we were already living together and after a year and a half while we were in Costa Rica on vacation, we celebrated our humanist wedding.

The Universe gave me a family beyond anything I could have dreamed of. Every time I see Joe, I see the perfection of the Universe. I see in him the palpable truth that magic exists, that everything we desire can materialize. I think about everything that had to happen to facilitate our encounter and bring into my life a man who, with his dedication and actions, has given my son so much self-confidence and allowed me to witness how the sweetest of dreams come true.

After our wedding, I started thinking about how I loved before and how I did now. Previously, all my relationships were passionate and intense, like one of those Latin soap operas where everything is drama, jealousy, and betrayal. The first time Joe and I met many years ago was one of the craziest episodes of my soap opera.

Even when we got back together, it was a bit intense. I was still crazy with jealousy and fought for little things. I guess I wanted to be in control of the relationship. Things changed so much after I started on this journey. Our love became sweet, clean, transparent, and profound.

I didn't feel as attached or demanding as in previous relationships. I loved him freely, and this was a newfound and incredible feeling. At first, I thought that losing that attachment meant not loving to the fullest, because in previous years I used to love him in a needy, crazy, and passionate way. But when I began to feel the connection with the Divine through my meditations, I experienced a love that was pure, open, and deep without any despair or need involved. Then, I was able to understand that the need for another person is not love, but quite the opposite. So today, I still love him with an open heart, as sincerely as I can, without expecting anything in return, and like magic, I end up receiving exactly what I have given.

The Wake-up Call

Before reconnecting with Joe, I ran two businesses at once. One involved managing properties, which I could do from home, and the other one consisted of a real estate brokerage, which I had recently started and which forced me to have a small office and several people who counted on me daily.

When I started the brokerage, I thought it would take me two or three years at most for it to run smoothly, without requiring much of my time. Actually, it could have worked like this, if I hadn't become obsessed with doing it all faster, and bigger. This obsession began to stress me. I was dedicating all my waking hours to this business, working more than humanly possible, but somehow I couldn't see it at that time.

Upon returning from Amsterdam in January 2017, I was trying to find the right people to delegate some responsibilities and avoid overworking, but this seemed increasingly difficult. In less than a month after returning, all the stress accumulated and was starting to make itself noticeable. I began to feel a terrible burden on my shoulders, and I became very depressed every time I stepped foot in the office.

I remember asking myself several times how I had put myself in that position, trying to do more than I could. I felt terrible for putting my health in jeopardy just to make more money when I was doing just fine before the brokerage.

All those days were a blur, since I couldn't pinpoint what was going on with me. I thought I was just overworked, and if I could find someone to take some of my responsibilities, everything would be okay. Thus, I decided to try to work from home, thinking that could help.

I've always been used to working hard, but this was different. My mind was totally taken over by the business. Over time, everything became more dreadful, and by the end, the effort was just unbearable, which forced me to think more carefully, analyzing the reason for the whole situation. Had everything become more difficult because it was not meant to be, or was that difficulty only part of the business, and I had to be more resourceful? Ahhh, the million-dollar question.

By now, you might have figured out that I was hard-headed back then, so of course, I thought the answer to that question was that I only needed to be more resourceful, so I continued working. This strategy didn't last very long, as one morning, while leaving home to go to the office, my mind suddenly went blank;

there was nothing inside it, no memories, no thoughts, absolutely nothing. For a few minutes, I was paralyzed in the middle of the kitchen, with the car keys in my hand, with full makeup on and fully dressed.

I started walking around the house to see if something came back to me, but nothing happened. I didn't know the time, the day, or the place where I was going, much less where I was. Then, after what seemed like an eternity and out of nowhere, I remembered my son, Troy, and I panicked. I looked at the clock to see if it was time for me to pick him up, but it was only around 9 a.m. With just him in my mind, I tried to relax, to calm the despair of not knowing what was happening. I sat on the bed waiting for something else to come back to me. I really don't know how much time passed, but little by little, my mind began to fill with all the memories I previously lost. It was as if my brain had restarted by itself.

After those minutes of mental emptiness, I realized that I could have lost it all. I could have remained in that state, blank and empty forever, and if that were to happen, it would not even be important how much money I was going to make that day, that week, or even that year.

I was woken up by my vulnerability. That mundane world where I was living seemed so irrelevant now. I was a single mother; I had a son who was counting on me to be there after school to pick him up day after day. How did I get to this point? How was I so disconnected from myself to walk down the wrong path for so long? Something was fundamentally wrong. It was as if I was living in a reality where my mind and my ego wanted to live, but not the reality "I" wanted to live.

Yes, the only things that kept me going in the wrong direction were my mind and my ego, both of which wanted more money and rejected failure. My mind had taken control over my life and was living the life it considered convenient for me to live. A life where I needed to earn more money, to have a better car, to gain respect, and to be admired. The real me just wanted to live a peaceful life and share it with my son, family, and friends.

All that depression, all that heavy weight on my shoulders I felt every time I went to the office, was the real "me" trying to wake me up, trying to show myself that I didn't want that life. The incident at home was also my body's little riot, a wake-up call.

I didn't even want to think about it anymore. I decided to close the business and take some time off. I couldn't let my mind keep making decisions for me. So, I decided not to get involved in anything until I was sure that it would take me on the right path. I continued working from home and only took care of my property management business.

I needed to relax, to let this madness disappear, and for some reason, for the first time in my life, I trusted the Universe to show me what to do next. I closed the office on April 1, 2017. We had already planned our summer vacations, and I thought that maybe by the time I returned, I would have some idea of what I was going to do next with my life.

4

WHEN THE UNIVERSE SHOWS YOU
THE WAY

WE HAD PLANNED our summer vacation at the beginning of 2017. Troy and I would spend 20 days visiting California with my family and then meet Joe and continue to Hawaii on a nine-day surf trip.

I had always wanted to go to California, so I was expecting it to be a memorable trip. I wanted to go with the right people to have the best memories. My dad had recently passed away, which made it a very emotional trip.

We visited most of the must-see spots in Los Angeles and drove along the coast to Santa Barbara. We passed through Big Sur until we got to San Francisco, and on the way back, we visited Napa Valley and Lake Tahoe, ending the tour in San Diego.

I had downloaded several audiobooks to listen to during the trip, one of which was a book called *The Surrender Experiment*, written by Michael "Mickey" Singer. I began listening to that book on the first day of the trip, and as simple as that, my beautiful journey to a Higher Consciousness had begun.

Listening to Mickey Singer talking about his experiences seemed surreal to me, as something very similar was happening in my life at that time. I had already surrendered and was taking some time off, waiting for the Universe to work its magic and show me the way.

Discovering Mickey's story while driving along the West Coast was a magical experience; it felt like this stranger invited me to join him in another world. I was completely hooked. That one was the first book that made me feel magic all over my body.

Mickey and his book both started to tease me into a world totally different from mine. He had chosen to live his life without worrying about how others said it should be lived. The prospect of such a different way of living kept me hungry for more, more of his work, and more of what moved him and supported him through his process.

I remember that in the days before this trip, I wanted to feel magic in my life. I wanted magic to guide my way, and there it was. I had received this beautiful gift from the Universe. That was the first magical moment of that summer, and since then, thousands of magical instances have flooded into my life.

A couple of days later, while reading another of Mickey's books entitled *The Untethered Soul*, I was drawn to *Autobiography of a Yogi* by Paramahansa Yogananda, a book that, according to Mickey, had changed his life.

When I started to read Yogananda's book, I can't say it was love at first sight. Not at all. It took me a while to understand it; at first, I attributed it to the British accent of the narrator and the Indian references on the Audible version. But even after obtaining a printed copy and beginning it, I noticed that it was the book itself that represented a challenge for me. I felt that Yogananda's work was well above my level of understanding, that it was too advanced for me. However, I didn't want to stop reading it. I wanted to discover what Mickey had found in it.

Instead, I came upon the statement that changed the course of my entire existence: "Kriya Yoga is a scientific method used to achieve enlightenment."

Once I unlocked the magic in Yogananda's book, I couldn't put it down. It captured me completely. The beauty of magic books is that everyone perceives something different when they read it. Personally, what I got from it, in addition to the sentence that changed my life, was understanding that you don't have to be special, mystical, or spiritually advanced to follow this path. In the book, Yogananda shares that he had lied when he was little trying to escape from his house, that he did not like to study, and was obsessed with mangoes and food like all of us. However, he still reached the supreme state of Samadhi, and not in a humble house in India next to the Ganges, but in his hermitage in Encinitas, California, one of the most spectacular places I have ever visited.

Gradually Yogananda's philosophy began to modify something in my head; the more I read, the more radiant I felt. I only read small fragments every day as I didn't want to finish it; I didn't want the magic to dissipate. Those little fragments made the trip much more meaningful. I deeply connected with every word that was written in them.

The day arrived when I had to meet up with Joe at the airport to continue to Hawaii. By the time I got there, I was about to finish the book, and I found myself carried by a state of profound bliss most of the time, where everything was perfect and magical. Nothing disturbed me. This was the way I wanted to feel forever. There was something coming out of those books that was already changing my perception of life.

Magic and Synchronicities on Elevated Paths

The Small Hawaiian café

There were two tiny magical events or synchronicities during that trip to Hawaii that helped me recognize that something in my life had changed, and allowed me to experience the magic that is always surrounding us.

The first of these events occurred on a day when we were returning from surfing on Waikiki Beach. I remembered being very disappointed by how commercial that part of Honolulu was. It seemed that you were anywhere in the world except in Hawaii. All businesses had been invaded by dozens of stores that sold exactly the same souvenirs, from T-shirts to mugs, all with the name "Hawaii" on them. The same happened with the restaurants and cafés; all were aimed at tourists who were forced to pay a premium for mediocre meals and poor service.

We had decided to stay there because it was the place with the best waves for beginners during the summer in Oahu. When we arrived at the lovely little Hawaiian bungalow that we had rented near the beach, it got into my head that Waikiki was missing an authentic small café on the beach where you could relax with good food and good music while enjoying the sunset.

After a shower and a well-deserved nap, we sat down to relax on the porch. It was a beautiful afternoon, one of those that promise amazing sunsets, so I felt the need to leave home and explore. It didn't take me long to convince Joe and Troy to go for a ride on our skateboards.

While skating, I felt inclined to go to a part of town that we hadn't yet visited, so we continued down the road and started following the sunset. After crossing a large park, we were able to see a quiet beach where the sun was setting. This part of the city seemed to be known only by the locals, as there were fewer people compared to the crowded streets of Waikiki that were only a few minutes away.

As we approached the beach to enjoy the sunset, we saw a small Hawaiian café with live music. The place was exactly as I had previously imagined, completely relaxed and unpretentious. We sat at a table a few feet away from the water, charmed by the music, the breeze, and the salty smell of the sea. The intense colors reflected by that sunset made that moment and that place somehow ethereal. I was enchanted by the coincidence, but still holding tight to my skepticism. It was going to take a bit more magic to make me a believer. Thus, a bit more of that magic was shown to me...

A Surprise Present

On the last day of our stay in Oahu, we decided to go to Whole Foods for a quick lunch. While driving there, my favorite song, "Talk of the Town" by Jack Johnson, one of the singers that Joe and I most admire, started playing in the car from my Spotify playlist.

The island vibes of the song reminded me that Jack Johnson was from Hawaii, specifically from Oahu, where we were staying. Then, for the rest of the ride, I contemplated the beautiful land-scape and began to daydream, imagining Jack Johnson walking on those streets. That dream didn't last long because the madness of finding a place to park quickly brought me back to reality.

Our day continued as usual; however, that night, while I was sitting on the porch, the breeze felt so delightful that it awoke within me the desire to go out to enjoy it fully.

We were so exhausted from our surf session that afternoon that we opted for a short walk instead of skating. It was our last night in Hawaii. The sun had already set, but for some unknown reason, we began to walk towards the same café we had found the day before.

To our surprise, a few blocks from the beach, the streets were blocked by police cars. When we asked the policemen, they told us there was a concert taking place in the amphitheater. As the streets were empty and there was no music playing, we figured out the show was about to start. I wanted to know who was playing, but the box office was far away. So we turned around to leave when suddenly I changed my mind and decided to check who was going to play.

I remember running quickly to the ticket office, and as I approached, I saw a banner that read "Jack Johnson." Instantly I started yelling at Joe: "Jack Johnson! Jack Johnson!" as I continued running like crazy.

As soon as I arrived and was able to catch my breath, I asked who was performing. Even when the cashier confirmed that it was Jack Johnson, I still couldn't believe it. I asked her if the concert was over, to which she replied that it was actually about to start, but that tickets were sold out.

I was baffled. How could the Universe send me there in the middle of the night, to not be able to be part of the concert? We looked around and saw a guy at the entrance selling some tickets. He had exactly three left! Joe opened his wallet and strangely had the exact cash the guy was asking for the tickets. And just like that, out of the blue, the most beautiful synchronicity of my life took place, allowing us to spend our last night in Hawaii at a Jack Johnson concert.

The whole night was a dream: the music, the breeze, the lights, and the energy of hundreds of people coming together under the starry sky of that island in the middle of the Pacific.

These were more than enough signs for me to know that I was on the right path to a Higher Consciousness. I really had no idea what to expect. Still, I realized that if the Universe had elaborated such a beautiful present for me in Hawaii, I was confident that it would continue to guide me through this process.

I didn't talk to Joe about that experience until recently when I asked him to recall some details with me, and for the first time, I felt comfortable enough to tell him what those events we lived together meant to me. He knew what books I was reading, and I had shared some of my experiences, but I had never told him about the significance of those events because I didn't want to scare him off. Things were happening very quickly. Little did I know that all that magic and all those synchronicities were only a very tiny fragment of all the wonders that I would be able to experience along this path.

A couple of hours after the Jack Johnson concert, I found myself running around the cute little Hawaiian bungalow, trying to fit all of our belongings into our luggage. We only had 30 minutes to finish packing and head towards the airport, but I couldn't help trying to catch a glimpse into Joe's eyes to see if he was still feeling the magic from last night. He knew what I was looking for, and every time my eyes met his, he shook his head in disbelief and continued trying to manage the chaos with a sweet smile on his face.

Troy was still sleeping. He had behaved like a trouper the night before at the concert with no complaints. I stopped for a second to contemplate him savoring his deepest dreams with his perfect little face and his perfect little open mouth. He was still lost into oblivion when I realized that the previous night's event had been the first concert of his life.

The moment had arrived for us to leave Hawaii. Joe carried Troy in his arms to the car. The full moon was still out, watching us sneak away to the airport.

From the highest point on Makapuu Avenue, I took my last glance at Waikiki. I looked down at the hills where I skated for the first time. As a backdrop to this last mental picture of Honolulu, I was given a pitch-black sky so intense that it made the full moon seem too big and too close to be real. The silhouette of the silent Diamond Head also appeared, claiming its importance, while the reflection of the gigantic moon danced in the now black waters of the beach, where Troy and I had ridden our first waves. It was the perfect, unwanted end of the magical vacation that divided my life into a before and after.

Lessons Learned

That night, as I left Hawaii and crossed the Pacific Ocean, I reviewed what I had learned from those trips and discovered that they both had helped me to corroborate three valuable lessons.

The first was the importance of stillness: to stay put, to give ourselves time, and to not force things to happen. I had been experiencing this since I closed my brokerage to let myself be guided by the Universe towards my next project.

While I was on that flight, I contemplated everything that had happened in the last few months. I couldn't help but thank the Universe, not only for rewarding me for waiting and showing me the path to follow but also for pushing me to live and experience that lesson. I had heard it a million times, to be patient, and to wait, but I had never actually done it, even though I had been presented with millions of opportunities to do so.

Most of my adult life, I felt like I was in a race in which I ran and ran with no idea of where the finish line was. That race always kept me exhausted, making me delay any enjoyment until I would reach the imaginary line that never appeared. Sitting there, looking out the window of the plane, I finally grasped the insanity of that race. I could clearly see that there was no finish line; that life was not a race, and therefore, there was no urge to get anywhere. There was no place in the future where my happiness was guaranteed. The sad truth was that all those years, I was running away from myself, from silence, from stillness.

Those last four months, from when I closed the brokerage until that day I left Hawaii, had been the time for me to face what I feared, whatever I was running away from. It was the time to stay still, to not get entangled in another drama. The goal was not only to stop running but also to wait and be patient, to give the Universe time to show me the path to follow.

On that day, suspended above blue waters and among cotton candy skies, I realized that at some point during those four months after I had stopped running, I was feeling comfortable in that state of inertia.

The second lesson was that the greatest gifts are not the ones we want to give ourselves but the ones orchestrated by the Universe. When we force things to happen or desperately jump in, we always fall short (as I did with the brokerage and my romantic relationships). We can never compete with the greatness of the Universe. All we can do is to wish with detachment (this is the keyword) and let the Universe work its magic and dazzle us with an infinitely improved version of what we asked for. I can't help feeling this every time I see Joe, every time I feel his love, and every time I let him feel mine.

The last lesson I received that summer thanks to reading Yogananda's *Autobiography of a Yogi*, was that you don't need to be a godlike human being, have special powers or a special connection with the Universe and the Creator, to see and feel magic or to walk on an enlightenment path. For some reason, after reading that book, something clicked within me, and I began to believe that we are all special, we can all feel magic and embark on a journey of spiritual enlightenment.

5

NEW BEGINNINGS

Returning Back Home

WE LANDED on a Sunday afternoon in Miami, exhausted by the twenty-four-hour aerial odyssey. However, the excitement of starting a new chapter in my life overcame the fatigue. I had the feeling that after that summer, nothing was going to be the same. The Universe had been gently guiding me to that moment in time where clouds that previously overshadowed my surroundings were gone, allowing me to clearly see that the scientific method of Kriya Yoga was the path to follow. Incorporating that practice into my life, and proving its effectiveness, was my next project, an endeavor that would give me the time and clarity needed to figure out what to do with my life.

I felt that everything was so well-orchestrated by the Universe, that the least I could do was to dedicate a full year to that practice in order to obtain valid results. I also planned to dedicate one hour to Kriya Yoga and another hour to journal about what happened to me before, during, and after the meditation. That journal was going to be the key to discover if any spiritual advancement had taken place within me. I needed to take my time with this project. I wanted to do it right. That was how my decision to take a semi-sabbatical year began to form.

Noticing the incredible shift in my life from being a real estate broker to a spiritual seeker in less than six months made me confident that once the Kriya Yoga project was finished, the Universe would again lead me onto another magical path. And I can't wait to transcribe in these pages the surprise the Universe gave me when that moment eventually came around.

Quitting Smoking

During the flight back to Miami, I decided to quit smoking as soon as I got home. The decision was made thinking mainly about my health, but I also felt it would help me to strengthen my will.

I remember asking myself: How can I follow a path of spiritual enlightenment if I am not even strong enough to control this addiction? Being honest, what tormented me the most was feeling unworthy of walking towards a Higher Consciousness because of all the damage I was causing to my body.

That same night, after landing in Miami, my crusade to quit smoking began, and thus the first entry in the journal was born:

> **Journal entry August 7, 2017:** Yesterday was my first night back in Miami, and my first night trying not to smoke. When I went out to the terrace to talk to Joe, as usual, he was smoking, and when he saw me, he offered me a cigarette. Before he offered it to me, I thought: Should I smoke? I had smoked a lot in Hawaii and already decided to quit. I think the hardest part was saying no the first time because after I did, I totally forgot that I needed to smoke.
>
> When Joe lit another cigarette, I expected him to offer me one, so my internal battle began: "Okay, just one more," I said to

myself while experiencing the feeling of relief I felt when I smoked. However, imagining how weak I would look in front of Joe, and knowing that after one I would have no strength to stop, I used every bit of strength in me to say no again when he offered a second smoke.

Today, almost two years have passed since that day. And if you would ask me if it was necessary to stop all my addictions before starting on this path, I would say no. I didn't need to quit smoking. I didn't have to prepare in any way or stop doing anything; I just needed to put my most sincere and honest effort into meditating, and everything else would come with the practice.

Our Self is formed by our essence, and that essence is something that we could never change, not even committing the worst of crimes. Our nature is pure, honest, and loving, a kind of eternal bliss. Therefore, as we move along this path and connect with that essence, everything that is not part of it will eventually disappear with less effort on our part.

So, when I was so desperately trying to stop smoking, all the stress and anxiety I created through forcing something to happen generated a spiraling pattern that kept me moving. This movement gave me a false sensation of going forward when, in reality, I was still trapped in the same place.

Journal entry August 24, 2017: Today I heard my brain saying: Well, I've been a good girl. I need a reward, so I wanted to smoke. What the hell? What a crazy idea. Why should I always try to release my stress or anxiety with food or cigarettes? This time, instead, I only drank my green tea, and I remembered that I only have to convince myself for that brief second when the thought crosses my mind. The best would be not to have these anxiety attacks, so I wouldn't have to try to convince my mind every time I want to smoke.

Today, when I go back to the journal pages where I was trying to stop smoking, I can actually feel the stress and anxiety. I remember not being able to control it; I smoked a few times after I decided not to. However, I rigorously continued with my meditations, until one day as if by magic, the urge and the anxiety disappeared. I no longer tried to deceive my brain or convince myself not to smoke; the realization that I was not a smoker was already part of me, and so everything else simply vanished.

Those moments, those precious vanishing seconds of realization in our lives, are nothing but presents given to us, with no explanation, no logic, no rules to follow. It doesn't matter if we are good or bad. Those seconds are nothing more than a manifestation of Higher Knowledge and glimpses of another level of consciousness.

Journal entry August 8, 2017: We came back from Hawaii two days ago. Today, Joe started getting up at 7 am to go to work. I felt madly guilty because I was still in bed, and you know how the mind works, I began feeling disgusted with myself for that laziness. The more I felt depressed, the less I wanted to get out of bed. I used this time to ponder, but pretty soon, I figured that I felt quite lost. I knew I wanted to try the scientific method to achieve enlightenment, but I didn't know how or where to start.

We are so used to having a teacher and a guide, that when we need to forge our own path, we don't know where to start. So, during those minutes in bed, I permitted myself to shape the next chapter of my life. I decided that the best time to start with Kriya Yoga was as soon as Troy began his new school year in late August.

By this time, my mind had woken up from its lethargy, and it was already bombarding me with its usual negative remarks... If enlightenment was that easy, many people would have already accomplished it, or What would you do if there is no change after losing an entire year? After listening to all of this nonsense in my head, and after two hours of feeling like nothing but manure, I started thinking that maybe I felt like this because I didn't have a concrete plan, so I jumped out of bed and began to work on it.

Semi-sabbatical Decision

One of the most challenging conclusions I reached during those early days of this path was realizing that I needed to slow down if I wanted to do things right. For me, this project was way more than just trying to meditate one hour a day to see if it worked while I continued my chaotic life waiting for a Higher Consciousness to fall from the sky and suddenly straighten out my whole life. No, I wanted more than that. I wanted to figure out if the method worked. And in order to do so, I needed to pause and study what was going on in my head every day during and after every meditation. Moreover, I wanted to document everything, and this would easily require two to three hours every day altogether.

At that moment, the idea I had during the flight back home flirted with me again. If I really believed that this project had been sent to me by the Universe, I had the obligation to take a leap of faith and dedicate myself to it with all my heart and time, which translated into not taking on new projects.

I was unable to take a proper sabbatical because I still owned the property management company, but I really wanted to take a year off. Looking back, it was a good thing that I didn't, because today I can see the value of being confronted every day with this mundane life: with tenants who complain, vendors that don't do their job, bills to pay, and people you have to be social with. Living in this man-made world while discovering a new one taught me much more than whatever I could have learned locked away in the Himalayas, untouched by chaos and imperfection. Here, every day, every situation, every reaction was a new case for self-study.

My Research into Kriya Yoga

After deciding to take a semi-sabbatical year, I started exhaustive research about Kriya Yoga. There was a lot of information on the subject, but for me, it was essential to stay close to the method taught by Babaji, who was the sage at the head of the Yogananda lineage.

Although many organizations professed to teach the "True Kriya Yoga," I only found two I felt comfortable with. Both organizations came from Babaji's lineage but differed in their teachings, methodologies, and practices.

The first organization was called Self-Realization Fellowship (SRF) and was founded by Yogananda. Its headquarters are located in Mount Washington, Los Angeles, California, but it has several locations worldwide. Its teachings are received in the form of lessons, sent by mail every two weeks. In addition, the student has to wait until a certain number of lessons to finally receive the one where the Kriya Yoga practice is explained.

Upon registering, I discovered that it would take an entire year for me to receive the lesson which explains the practice of Kriya Yoga, and there was no way to speed up the process. Despite not being comfortable with the time frame, I registered and received their lessons biweekly. I remember always anticipating their arrival in the mail.

The other organization was founded by Paramahamsa Hariharananda and is called Kriya Yoga International Organization

(KYIO). Today, this organization is led by the spiritual successor of Hariharananda: Paramahamsa Prajnanananda, and it also has several centers around the world. To my surprise, the mother center was located in Homestead, Florida, forty-five minutes from Miami.

According to them, the Kriya Yoga technique must be transmitted from master to disciple, master to aspirant, or teacher to student during an initiation. They firmly believe that all the teachings come from the actual practice; therefore, they don't offer lessons or have gurus to follow after the initiation.

In the beginning, I didn't like the idea of walking on the path of enlightenment alone. But, after more than two years of practice, I can see how this uncommon aspect of the organization fosters its benevolence. This path is so intrinsically ours that no one else will be able to lead us through it. It is a journey within ourselves, a way to realize our essence, to connect with our uniqueness, and with it all. Only the practice will show us the way; no one else will.

Today, I have come to respect and appreciate both organizations. Even though I received the lessons from the SRF, I did not practice the Kriya Yoga taught by them because I was initiated by KYIO earlier and had amazing results from the continued practice of their technique. I visit the KYIO mother center in Homestead almost every Sunday for the group meditations, their fantastic vegetarian lunch, and to be surrounded by Hariharananda's energy.

As this center is close to home, I have more contact with its members and remain very involved; I do a little Seba (volunteer work) and hear about the new monks' experiences. They have become my meditation family, and a place where I don't need to talk to anyone. I just show up, meditate and smile, and that has been more than enough for me.

6

MY REGULAR MEDITATIONS

My First Regular Meditations

IN AUGUST 2017, I enrolled in both Kriya Yoga organizations. The next initiation at KYIO's mother center in Homestead would take place on October 14. I was so avid and ready to start that those two months seemed like an eternity. Thus, I decided to start practicing on my own, committing to meditate every day for 30 minutes, as a kind of training until the "big day" arrived. Everything seemed like a great idea, although I had a small problem: I had no idea how to meditate.

I had tried more than fifteen years ago while reading a practical meditation book entitled *The Monk Who Sold His Ferrari*, written by Robin S. Sharma. Without any exaggeration, I can tell you that in those days, I tried to meditate more than twenty times, but I felt like such a freak and a loser every time I tried. I couldn't keep my mind still, not even for a second. I remember that I kept trying because I felt the practice possessed some magic within. However, I did not know if I was progressing, so I simply stopped practicing after a while.

I wish, during those first attempts, I had known that meditation is nothing more than a solo trip and that there is no right or wrong way to do it. What is essential is finding "your way" to do it. Meditation is not only those elusive seconds of nothingness, but your process to get there, because those times when you think it isn't working are the times when all the progress is made.

This time around, I tried to keep it simple. I didn't want to go on YouTube to find one of those "I know it all" kinds of people that confused me with weird ideas. I wanted to do it in the most authentic way possible. I knew that my mind just needed to be still, so that was all I planned to do. And so, without further instructions, that same day, I sat in a half-lotus position, set the alarm for 30 minutes, closed my eyes, and began.

> **Journal entry August 10, 2017:** I set my alarm for thirty minutes, but I only meditated fifteen because I was desperate to finish. During the entire meditation, I could hear all kinds of noises, even noises that have always been there but that I have never paid attention to, were now extremely distracting. Everything got me off track. I also realized that I have to do it earlier, in the morning, before everything else so that there are fewer things on my mind. I will not stress. I will be patient.

The next day I meditated only for twenty minutes. This time I blamed it on (as I wrote in my diary) "that b**** in high heels that lives in the apartment above."

> **Journal entry August 12, 2017:** Today, I meditated for ten minutes only, but I was calmer than all of the previous times. I realized that meditation is something very personal. It is a journey that you must take on your own because only you can discover its meaning.

Journal entry August 13, 2017: Today, I started with five breaths, sitting in a half-lotus position. Thoughts didn't want to leave, and the more I thought they had to leave, the more stressed I became, and the less I could meditate. Finally, I relaxed and realized that I had to let go and surrender to the experience. By then, the alarm went off, and I was happy to be done.

Journal entry August 15, 2017: I am still working on perfecting my meditation. Today it was irregular as usual. But I noticed that I am so in love with this practice that I created a way to make it totally mine. I did everything to be more comfortable, ready, and present. I started using some incense, made some movements and adjustments that helped me with my back and bowed. Then, it was as simple as sitting in a half-lotus position, with the back of my hands on my knees, waiting until I became calmer and more grounded so I could begin with my meditation.

To be honest, when I started, many thoughts came to my mind. However, I have noticed that with practice, they have reduced the length of their stay. I also see that now when they appear, I don't get stressed or angry, like I used to. I choose to believe that this is normal and that everybody new to this practice would encounter the same obstacle.

Something that helped me a lot was applying the following technique: as soon as a thought appeared in my mind, I didn't get engaged with it, I didn't ask why it appeared or get angry. I simply imagined that thought flying away from me, and I repeated this every time any distraction invaded my mind. Sometimes I didn't realize that I got involved with a thought, but once I noticed it, I applied the same technique; I watched it fly away and continued with my meditation. With time and practice, there were fewer and fewer thoughts in my head.

I continued with my thirty-minute daily meditation for the next two months. I was very consistent. I remember skipping it only three times during those sixty days, and every time I sat down to practice, I was rewarded with something different, something unique, something beautiful. Yet, I never imagined that from this simple practice, I would soon receive many dazzling presents.

Self-Studies

The self-studies that began to appear in my journal were milestones on my way to a higher consciousness. They were situations that caused me tremendous confusion, a downpour of tears, and immense pain, yet they guided me to places within me that I had always run away from—my attachments to the mundane world.

As time went by and the situations that caused my self-studies were resolved, much of what clouded my vision and kept me tied to a world without magic dissipated, making me much lighter. I was stripped from burdens that were never mine, so I could finally see who I really was.

I have included an Afterword at the end of the book, where I share, based on my experiences, how meditation works. I recommend reading that excerpt as many times as needed from this point forward as it will facilitate the understanding of many of the self-studies contained in the following pages.

My Attachment to Money – Self-Study

My attachment to money was the first milestone on my path towards higher consciousness. The turmoil began during the first week of my semi-sabbatical year when my biggest challenge was not to get involved with any extra work.

In the past, the money coming from my property management business was money that was saved. It wasn't used to cover my expenses. I always subsisted on the money I produced from my real estate deals. Therefore, not being able to make money with real estate meant that I had to live off "my savings." I was very disturbed by not making the money I was used to making, and that feeling of loss began to cause me a lot of anxiety.

I have never denied that money was my priority in those days, becoming almost like an addiction. Most of the people around me, including friends and family, share a similar perspective regarding money. Thus, everyone close to me believed I had lost my mind when I first mentioned my decision to take a semi-sabbatical year. Undoubtedly, all of them made the same calculations as I did, estimating how much money I would lose pursuing this path.

I reached my lowest point regarding this issue one day after coming home from my yoga class:

> **Journal entry August 16, 2017:** Today, I returned from yoga at noon, feeling like a loser, as if I had wasted my entire morning doing nothing productive. I felt so miserable, and like such a parasite. My mornings nowadays consist of meditation, writing in my diary, and going to the Ashtanga Yoga studio nearby. For the first time in my life, I felt like I had no value as a person because I was not producing all the money I could.
>
> With that last thought hovering in my head, I couldn't hold it in any longer, so I collapsed in the middle of my living room and began to cry. There was no way to stop me, and frankly, I didn't want to do it either. I had this pressure building up in my chest for so long that it was making me ill, and I needed to let it out.
>
> My heart was torn. I felt that I was doing the right thing, but my mind was screaming at me that I was a fool. Who would say

no to making more money? I thought for a second, but I couldn't find anyone that would say "no" to making more money. So I continued crying. After a while, there were no more tears coming out. I was just there lying on the carpet, staring at the ceiling totally exhausted. I spent several hours there, trying in vain to find a solution to my distress until the phone rang, and I got stuck with property management stuff until I had to pick up Troy from school.

As the days went by, my meditations became unstable. Some days, my mind could go blank for what seemed like five minutes; others, not even for a second. Frankly, I didn't care much about it, because when I managed to silence my mind even for one second, the sensation was sublime. However, the money issue was still there.

Journal entry August 19, 2017. I really need this. I need to give myself this time in exchange for all the hard work I have done my whole life. I need to discover who I am and not what I am supposed to do with my life. I am tired of using my time to make money and never feel fulfilled. I imagine that if I know myself a little more, finding my purpose in life would come naturally. There must be something more out there! Life shouldn't be wasted on activities that don't move us or that we even hate, just to get money, and this is how I currently feel with my property management business. I have made many mistakes in choosing my path in the past; this time, I will let the Divine guide me to my next chapter. I am taking this time to connect with myself spiritually, mentally, and physically. These are my treasures, and I want to cultivate them.

Journal entry August 22, 2017. This makes no sense! Although one of my wishes for this year was to work for only two or three hours a day, now that I can afford that luxury, I don't feel happy. There must be something very, very wrong with me! How many people would be happy to work just a couple of hours to support themselves? EVERYONE.

This terror of not having enough money forces me to believe that I must work every second of my day, even doing things that I hate doing. The fact is that I was born into a family with few resources and was educated with a "working hard" mentality; thus, I've been doing precisely that my whole life. It is almost impossible for me to believe in a life without strenuous effort or fear of tomorrow's uncertainties like this path suggests.

I found more journal entries related to this self-study, but I only selected the few that summarized the issue and how I felt about it. In those days, I had no idea how to solve the problem, because I didn't even know what the problem was.

The idea of being attached to making money and to money itself could not register in my mind, but that was precisely what was happening. One of the definitions of attachment is "an extra part or extension." And that was precisely what was going on. I believed that money was a part of who I was. Therefore, it became intrinsically related to my value as a person: the more money I had and produced, the more worthy I became. On the contrary, if I produced or had less money, immediately my value decreased, to a point where I could feel totally worthless and useless.

The only good thing about attachment is that it starts to vanish once you become aware of it. So, as I began to notice my attachment, the number of journal entries where money and work were mentioned began to decrease until one day, they disappeared altogether.

Today, money is not in my mind unless I think about it intentionally. I see it merely as a means for transactions to take place so the man-made world can continue to exist. I am fully detached from it. The money in my bank account or the monetary value of my assets has no relation to who I am. Before, I was so attached to it that I felt like I was losing a part of myself when I paid for something. I always knew exactly how much I had, so when I could buy what I wanted, I felt successful and happy. But when the opposite happened, I felt like a loser, got depressed, and worked harder for more.

Sometimes, I reflect on a question that always made me tremble: What would happen if I lost all my money and possessions? Today, I can answer honestly. I will still have my meditation, and with this, I have the power to live in a world that fills me with peace and harmony any time I close my eyes and quiet my mind. Even if I were living under a bridge or doing a job that barely allowed me to survive, I would still be able to close my eyes for a few minutes and be the most blissful woman on earth. That's something that money has never done for me.

Seeing Money as Energy

As the months passed, and my consciousness began to rise, a door opened within me that led me on the verge of the physical world I was so used to seeing and feeling. There, I began to grasp that everything that exists in this Universe is simply energy. Going beyond that door caused a structural change in many aspects of my life, including the one that formed my perception of money.

Today I see money simply as energy, and as energy, it is neither bad nor good. Most of the time, we work tirelessly to force this energy towards us, even though there are more harmonic ways to attract this energy, using higher forces such as inspiration.

Before Kriya Yoga, I had never been in direct contact with inspiration, but today I couldn't live without it. I used to have that old-fashioned idea that love and passion for what you do would give you the riches of the Universe. Today, I understand that love lacks drive. Although passion might somehow compensate for the idleness of love, it will always lead us towards attachment. Inspiration, on the other hand, contains those two magic ingredients: the love and the drive. Inspiration is what makes the impossible possible; it is the magic of creation and the force of attraction.

Today, when others ask me if I want to have or make more money, I simply answer that I don't pursue money. Somehow, traveling on this path has given me the certainty that I will always have what I want and need as long as I welcome inspiration to my life. I have finally understood that this force is the only one with the keys to all the wealth in the Universe.

Following the Path Through the Chaos – Self-Study

When I started this path, I wanted to find peace, joy, happiness, and a connection with myself and my body, but I still felt like one of the worst people in the world. I could still feel the suffering, the pain, and my slavery to harmful acts. Although none of these were too strong, they were still there, present, always pulling me down while I made an enormous effort to keep getting up and keep on walking.

I remember feeling so ready for all that to disappear. It was like a background noise that didn't allow me to concentrate on my practice. Over time, I discovered that my life is a reflection of my meditation, and my meditation is a reflection of my life. Now, whenever the suffering, harmful acts, or bad thoughts are back in my life, I do the same as in my regular meditations. I just see them floating, disappearing into nothingness, without feeling stressed or anxious. I don't get involved with them or wonder why they are here or why they don't leave. I just let them float far away from my mind, and I do my best to simulate that meditative state while living my life.

Experiencing Absolute Bliss

After three weeks of practicing my regular meditations, I began to experience a feeling of absolute bliss. I didn't notice a difference between the absolute bliss that I experienced during these regular meditations and what I experienced later when I started practicing my Kriya Yoga meditations. However, I couldn't honestly say whether I would have reached the level of consciousness I am at now with only the regular meditations.

My first experience of absolute bliss:

> **Journal entry September 2, 2017:** I have not meditated in the last two days, so today, when I sat down to meditate, I was a little apprehensive. I thought that I was going to be punished for not meditating, or that I was going to be so out of shape that I wouldn't be able to keep my mind steady. I started with five breaths in a half-lotus position. My thoughts didn't want to let go, and I knew that the more I forced them to leave, the more I would get stressed, and less meditation would be done.
>
> So finally, I relaxed and sincerely surrendered to the experience. I immediately felt as if my whole body was slowly melting away. I knew that my body was still there, although I was not able to feel it. All the noise that surrounded me before was somehow far away, and I was ultimately unaffected by it. My mind was not thinking about the woman in high heels on the floor above or calling the plumber to fix the noise in the toilet.
>
> Suddenly, the air had reached such a perfect temperature that it seduced my body to become more like it. I had the feeling of holding on to something that didn't allow me to let go completely, so I consciously decided to surrender to the experience. And when I did, I felt like I was floating into nothingness. Curiously, my body was not the one suspended in that weightlessness. It was my being who invisibly drifted into

oblivion, and as it did, I could feel waves of absolute bliss taking over. It all felt so sweet and so delicate that I wanted to hold on to that sensation forever.

Those experiences of absolute bliss are for me like little diamonds that I find along the way; they are so full of magic that I could describe them a million times, and each description would be entirely different. I see them as waves that maintain their beauty and charm, locked in their uniqueness. At first, they began to appear as timid sparks, and for me, those shy sparkles meant everything. They were my first contact with another reality, my connection with another world.

These bliss experiences kept me in awe every time they appeared. With time and perseverance, those sparks stopped being shy, lengthening their stay, and giving me the sweetest states of being—but of course—they were never enough. I quickly became obsessed and wanted to experience them every time I meditated, yet I had no control over them. Sometimes, that absolute bliss was peacefully waiting for me, but most of the time, it was me who anticipated its presence in my meditations, without being rewarded by its arrival. In those days, I tried everything. I tried to meditate every day, more diligently, and for more extended periods of time. I did everything I thought could work, but I got nothing. Until one day, I gave up and accepted that those experiences were presents that worked as mysteriously as the Universe itself, and so I let them come and go as they pleased.

Experiencing Absolute Love

Journal entry September 23, 2017: My niece, Annabelle, was born today. I was deeply moved and connected with that moment and its meaning, elevated by the transcendental aspect of the most natural thing in the world. Nothing else mattered after receiving the news. It was as if the whole world had stopped. The only important thing was that this little person had finally appeared in our world as one of us, a part of our family for the rest of our lives. Carried by this feeling, I began to write a letter to my sister-in-law to share with her how grateful I felt to have her as part of our lives and our family.

While writing that letter, I suddenly felt something sublime: my being contained an ethereal substance that I did not recognize because it wasn't gas, water, or solid. Instead, this substance was formed of glittering energy that attuned me to the entire Universe. It was like being full of invisible clouds that made me levitate, even though my body was still connected to the earth, motionless and in the same place.

The only thing I could see, feel, breathe, and hear was that substance that was inside me. I didn't have to think about what it was, because I somehow knew it: it was love, in its purest and absolute form. Strangely, this pure love hadn't just arrived; I had the inkling that it has always been here, within me, but somehow, I was never able to connect with it until that moment.

The experience was so intense, so sublime, and so out of this world, that it is impossible to explain it with words. However, daring to make from the ethereal the mundane, I would describe it as the sum of all the most intense moments of happiness, love, and ecstasy that I have experienced throughout life, multiplied to infinity. These were the most sublime twenty minutes of my life. The ecstasy I experienced was so intense that it made my entire body vibrate with a radiant and inexhaustible exaltation. I was also able to perceive how the waves of love that flooded my being couldn't contain themselves and overflowed, spreading through everything around me.

The sweetness and delicacy of that love carried me to new heights, and from there, the world seemed to be this majestic and perfect place where everything moved slower. It was the absolute bliss coming from this pure love what filled me with so much certainty that anchored me to the present moment.

I knew that pure love I felt was the energy that exists within everything: our breath, the sea, the earth, the trees, within all of us. That pure love is what moves everything, what makes magic happen, and what materializes our dreams—it is the Supreme Power.

The feeling remained with me for a period that seemed like hours. It was unlike any other state previously experienced. I was entirely sure that there wasn't a more intense feeling than that, except for Samadhi, which is the divine state in which the human consciousness becomes one with the cosmos. I noticed when that pure love began to dissipate because although I could still feel myself levitating and radiant, the waves of love ceased to pour out of me.

How could this pure love have always been here inside, without me being able to feel it? That experience was like finding a secret passage that allowed me to look inward. I tried to hold on to all of it as much as possible while trying to discover how it happened, how could I make it stay forever, or at least prolong it. I was worried that I could never feel that pure love again.

All of my efforts were in vain because little by little, the sensation faded, and the connection was lost. And when this happened, it seemed as if another "me" had taken my place.

This new "me" was pushing me to stress and worry about everything mundane: for getting the right flowers, for deciding how to dress, for what I was going to say, and for trying not to be late. Each new concern seemed even more important than the previous one, and suddenly I found myself trapped in this other world totally opposite to the one I was experiencing a few minutes ago.

At that moment, I was so absorbed and immersed in all the madness that had taken hold of me, that I couldn't analyze why such different experiences could result from the same situation.

However, now that we've returned from the hospital and I am able to write this journal entry, I realize that what I felt earlier was an openness in my heart, an openness that I was ready to commit to forever chase, as I now know what it holds.

Meditation as a Way to Open the Heart

Today, more than a year has passed since Annabelle's birth, and while integrating the previous journal entry into the book, I couldn't help crying when reliving those precious seconds of pure love. I feel fortunate to have been able to live such profound and beautiful experiences that have guided me through the expansion of my consciousness to new and unexplored territories.

When I was working on one of the several drafts of this section of the book, I asked Joe to read it to see his perspective. One of the comments that surprised me most was: "I have thirteen nieces and nephews, whom I love deeply, but I had never felt something so intense when they were born," and I would like to use his opinion to clarify what happened that day.

That transcendental experience of pure love was not only produced by Annabelle's birth. All of the previous weeks of meditation, and all of my efforts to expand my consciousness also played a crucial role. I feel as if, somehow, all of it had opened a channel of communication with my being, my consciousness, and the Divine, and through that channel and that connection, I could now live and experience dazzling truths.

Truths that began as simple states of absolute bliss, and that on that September day, evolved to new heights.

Ever since that day, I have found myself secretly wishing to be able to perceive that pure love again. However, it has never returned, so I only have moments like this when I reread these lines and evoke the beauty of that experience.

7

THE WELCOME OF KRIYA YOGA TO MY LIFE

Kriya Yoga: My Definition

I HAD WAITED to practice Kriya Yoga for more than two years, to have insightful knowledge about this practice and specifically the one taught by KYIO.

I perceive Kriya Yoga as a straightforward but robust technique that has been developed and improved through centuries by sages who hold immeasurable knowledge on this subject. It comprises several exercises and systems that are the key to the enormous enlightenment power it conveys. Through its exercises, Kriya Yoga creates new avenues to take us inward, avenues that with simple meditation would take years to develop. That's why I always refer to Kriya Yoga as "meditation on steroids."

When I began to practice, every detail and every exercise seemed very strange; As time passed, I slowly discovered the meaning and importance of each of them. The objective in the practice of Kriya Yoga is a spiritual one and arises from Raja Yoga, one of the branches of yoga where the union of our individual spirit with the Divinity is the primary aim. I have personally practiced Kriya Yoga only once a day for an hour straight.

However, it is said that better results are achieved when one-hour sessions are held twice daily.

The story of Kriya Yoga is beautifully explained in *Autobiography of a Yogi*, where it is said to have been known in ancient India but got lost until 1861 when Mahavatar Babaji introduced it to Lahiri Mahasaya. From then on, this technique was passed down through an unbroken lineage of masters taught via guru-disciple relationships in an initiation.

The Initiation to Kriya Yoga According to KYIO

KYIO has been my spiritual oasis, nestled in the jungle, enduring hurricanes, floods, and the passing of the years. It has always remained undisturbed and hidden enough to prevent the mundane from corrupting it, but still present, willing to share one of the most beautiful gifts in the Universe.

As I walk through its gardens, I get to feel this raw, uncontrolled, and non-manipulated beauty. There, you won't be able to find meticulously manicured spaces or exotic flowers. On the contrary, you will find something sweeter than that, which is the result of the effort, love, and gratitude of the attendees, who return everything received by this practice with the maintenance of those spaces. And this simple beauty is so real that I find it to be the perfect combination of nature, love, and care.

I remember that since the first day I entered the KYIO Homestead Ashram, I was trying to find "the trap." I was always waiting for them to try to brainwash me into believing that a tithe was a must so my meditations could be more fruitful, or waiting for them to request a monetary contribution. Yet, in the two years that I have regularly attended the Sunday group meditation, I have never had anyone come up to me asking for something. Instead, that center has given me the most transcendental gifts of my existence.

KYIO does not belong to the superficial world that we inhabit, and this fact is so rare that sometimes I am mundanely tempted to keep it as my little secret, not telling anyone about it. However, when I reach my elevated states, I know that everyone has to know about them because this humble organization really practices what it preaches, which is nothing else but love and union. Therefore, it has, without a doubt, earned my utmost respect and my most sincere appreciation.

Initiation Day

The initiation into Kriya Yoga consists of an introductory conference, followed by the initiation ceremony given by an approved Yogacharya, ending with three follow-up guided group meditations. After the initiation, practitioners have all the tools and knowledge to meditate regularly on their own. However, they can also attend group meditations in their area, depending on their availability (usually weekly).

The initiation weekend had arrived, and I did not know what to expect. I had been struggling with the word "initiation" since I had signed up for it two months ago. To me, that word sounded like something coming from a cult, and what went through my mind when I thought about it was brainwashing, orgies, rapes, etc. Then, you can imagine how apprehensive I was on my way to the Ashram that Saturday.

Hurricane Irma had passed recently, and its raging path of destruction was noticeable in all the vegetation surrounding the place. The ashram stood there unassuming, clashing immediately with the typical Miami flashy style. I parked in the designated area and started my way through the pathway, late as usual.

Once at the front door, I took off my shoes and walked in, following the voices as I explored the unfamiliar place. My mind was making substantial efforts to analyze every bit of information in order to label the place. I looked around, trying to take everything in, but I soon realized that a label was impossible as I had never been in a place like this before.

As soon as I opened the door to where the voices came from, I found myself in the meditation hall where everyone gathered. The ceremony had just begun. The saffron-clad teacher seated in the middle of the room pointed to the cushion on the floor that was reserved for me.

As the ceremony started, we pledged to keep everything we learned during the initiation to ourselves and not share it with others. Thus, I will share my personal experience and the fragments of the ceremony that are already open to public knowledge—through the KYIO website.

I can't deny that I was extremely nervous. I didn't know what to expect, yet I can't deny that I was hoping to feel something. Having read *Autobiography of a Yogi*, I expected great experiences of absolute bliss, messages from the other side, anything.

The teacher began with a sacred ceremony to purify the spine and the senses of the body. Shortly after, he started a process to infuse the three divine qualities. Through this phase, the seeker learns to perceive the inner light of the soul, to hear the divine sound, and to feel the divine movement sensation all over the body. We were supposed to experience, if not all three, at least some of them.

When my turn came, I quite freaked out. My heart started to race. I wanted so badly to escape from that situation. But, when the moment arrived, and the teacher placed his hand over my head, the divine sound "Om" flooded my whole being. I was completely incredulous about what I was experiencing.

Surprisingly, the sound vibrating within me was not new to me. I had had access to it many times in the past while I was in the forest, alone, surrounded only by nature, and away from the mundane.

The teacher kept looking at me, waiting for an answer while I was absorbed in my reminiscences. After a few seconds, I simulated the "Om" that resonated within. No words came out of his mouth. He just nodded with a smile escaping from his lips and continued the ceremony.

Since that day, that divine sound accompanies me every day. I just have to close my eyes and concentrate on it, to be able to hear it. Somehow I have the certainty that this "Om" will always be here within me, unalterable and always divine.

I was not able to perceive the other two divine qualities during the initiation ceremony. It took several months of Kriya Yoga practice for me to be able to perceive them. During that time, I learned to be patient. Some days, those divine qualities tried to reveal themselves to me but then dissipated in the idleness of my meditation. But, with only that quick of a flirt, I felt more enamored than before. Until one day, they finally let themselves be felt.

The rest of the day included blessings with flowers and oblations of breath to the fire—symbolic ceremonies that allow cleansing to happen at more subtle, and more profound levels, where the depth of purification depends upon the desire and receptivity of the seeker. Only after all the ceremonies were conducted was the ancient technique of Kriya Yoga explained to us.

At the end of the first day, I was exhausted by all the learning and by trying to do everything correctly. Nonetheless, I couldn't ignore the fact that Kriya Yoga was not merely a meditation technique, but also a spiritual practice, since its essence not only revolves around the exercises but also around the belief (or faith) in God, without following any religion.

At that time, I used terms such as Higher Power or Higher Consciousness that represented the Creator and were more aligned with what I had felt during my humble elevated states. Therefore, I decided to remain honest with myself and replace the word "God" with "Higher Power" when I meditated. That is how, since that Sunday, I have practiced every day with the purest honesty and sweetest love.

When I look back and evoke that weekend, I recognize the magnitude of the present I received that day. I understand the significance of the initiation and why a Master infusing you with the divine qualities is needed. Everything I experienced that weekend validated my belief: "We can't find magic with mundane methods."

My Take on Masters and Gurus

During the Kriya Yoga meditation practice, there is a section where you thank the masters who have transmitted this practice through the years. This represented a great challenge for my skeptical mind, as I did not feel any love or connection to them, and I believe that I would never reach the level of devotion and love that I saw in many of the practitioners who visited the ashram during that Initiation weekend.

Nevertheless, I was not going to allow myself to be discouraged by such a small detail, so I kept practicing with an open heart. Inexplicably, as my meditations continued, I began to grow fond of those teachers, and by the time I could notice my progress, my heart was already filled with immense gratitude towards them.

Over time, the path became more and more difficult. It would have been much easier to stop meditating, but I continued. During those times, I asked those masters for the strength I needed to continue on this path. I knew they had also endured the same difficulties. So I created a short ritual at the beginning of each meditation, where I bowed and thanked them with the deepest and most sincere love.

One day, I remember feeling the desire to make a small altar in the room where I always sat to meditate, and while I was thinking about what to put on the altar, I came up with the idea of placing an image of each master. However, I believed that if they wanted to be at my altar, they would have to come to me; I would not look for them.

So, when next Sunday arrived I visited the ashram in Homestead to meditate as usual. At the end of the session, I got interested in one of the books they were selling at the little ashram store, not thinking much about it; I just bought it. Yet, during the week, while I was lying in bed reading it, I started to look through the pages, and right in the middle of the book, I found cut-out pictures of each one of the eight masters. Baffled but excited, I immediately cut them out and placed them in the space I had already designated, and thus began my altar.

Today I feel the same sincere and deep love for all those masters. They represent the link between this new world that I am discovering and the mundane world I live in. I honestly cannot help feeling that they are the ones who have enlightened me and guided me to this day through their books and all the knowledge they accumulated and transmitted for generations.

I also remember that at one point, I had wanted a flesh and blood guru to guide me, thinking that this would make my path smoother. So I would go to the ashram in Homestead, expressing some of my concerns to the monks who live there. However, their response to every question I asked was always, "Keep practicing."

At first, I can't deny I got a bit frustrated. I had so much stuff going on in my head and so many questions. Still, the answer was always the same, "Keep practicing." Over time, I realized that answer was the only valid one because there is nothing someone can tell you or show you that is more revealing than a good meditation practice.

From that moment on, it became clear to me that my guru was none other than myself. The best advice that I can give if you start any enlightenment path is to look inside yourself every time you need advice or guidance. If the answer is not there, it will naturally come with practice. Be your own guru. When we get disconnected from our true selves, we become very vulnerable, and there are many people out there ready to take advantage of that situation.

The moment we believe in another person more than in ourselves, we are giving our power away. Do not give your power to anyone. We are all human beings. We are all the same. We all have the same power to connect with divinity. We just have to meditate, meditate, and meditate, and we will experience the Divine firsthand... and that is way more than any sermon we could hear.

8

ADVANCES WITH KRIYA YOGA

The Pendulum Effect

THE FOLLOWING MONDAY, after my initiation weekend, something bizarre happened. It was an experience that will always remind me of the person I used to be, as well as all the anger that had accumulated for years inside me.

That Monday, I needed to stop by the Hialeah City Hall to pick up some documents. It was a beautiful day, and I got there very early in the morning. My best guess is that in those days, I believed I was "The Queen of Hialeah" because when I noticed that there were no parking spaces available, I decided to block two cars that were legally parked. I was going to be in and out in no time and thought it wasn't going to be a big deal.

While I was running from the parking lot to the City Hall entrance, a man smoking by the door of the building started walking towards me, yelling that I couldn't park there. As he approached me, he began to scream even louder, making some crazy gestures with his hands. The screams were so rambunctious that everyone around turned to look at him.

When the man was close enough, I noticed he was wearing a uniform from the City of Hialeah, but it wasn't the one worn by the security guards. I started walking back to my car, trying to get away from the crazy guy, but instead of getting in my car and leaving, I faced him and yelled at him in a challenging tone. "Who are you? Do you work with the security of the parking?" I was sure that no security guard would act that crazy. As he got close enough, I was able to see the logo of his shirt that read: "City of Hialeah- Maintenance" At that moment, I lost it and blew the whole episode out of proportion.

I started yelling at him in a derogatory tone that he should go to clean the toilets instead of pretending to be a security guard. Right then, the guy who was not at all in his right mind lost what little sanity he had left as he pounced on me. I quickly got in my car and closed the door in his face while laughing at him from the safety of my car. My amusement didn't last too long because soon enough, the man pulled something out of his nose and smeared it on the window of my car—he was definitely unhinged.

Today the whole situation sounds hilarious to me, but not at that time. Well, at least not for the two of us. I decided to wait until a space became available to park my car and do my errand, thinking the aspiring security guard would soon get tired and leave. But when he noticed that I had decided to stay, he became even crazier and started yelling that he would call the police to get me arrested. A normal person would have left this altercation up to that point. It was evident that the man wasn't sane. But I was not normal...well, not at that time. I was totally blinded by fury and by the way the madman was acting. I burst into a mocking laughter, and I yelled at him that he could never get me arrested, that it was impossible, that he was an ignorant who didn't know the law. Finally, I gave him the finger.

The situation was insane. I couldn't get out of my vehicle because I was afraid the madman would do something to me or the car, but I didn't want to leave either. I kept wondering how he could act like that when the most important question was: How could I behave like that? It was a scene straight out of a cheap movie, and I was starring in it.

When the police arrived, I told them my version of the story and went inside to find the paper I needed. I was already parked in one of the designated spaces, and of course, the police couldn't do anything. With all the madness of that man, I had lost two hours of my day, so I was extremely upset.

I asked the officer who was writing the report to give me the name of the guy so that I could file a complaint with the city, and the guy started to freak out. The police officer asked me to leave, but I was so upset that I began to act in a very despotic way. I told the policeman that I was paying my taxes for them to be taking criminals off the streets and for the guy to clean the toilets not for wasting TWO HOURS in a crazy fight with me, a taxpayer who paid for their salary. Finally, I got in my car and left.

Upon returning home, I began to realize what had just happened. I was still totally enraged. It was the first time in my life that I had acted that way, entirely blinded by anger. What made the situation even more disturbing was the fact that I had just spent the whole weekend in the ashram getting initiated.

I sat on the couch in my house for a long time, merely looking for an answer that could explain my behavior. Why had I exploded like that? How could this enlightenment process work backward? The more I thought about it, the less coherent my answers became. The event was so bewildering to me that I could not wrap my head around it. After a few days, I just dropped it, thinking that it wouldn't happen again. But of course, similar explosions happened several times after that, not as intense or dramatic, but still pretty mind-boggling because they were unexpected and totally out of my control.

After writing about many of these experiences in my journal and after doing an in-depth self-study, I began to notice that shortly after having the most beautiful and intense experiences of connection with the Divine, I would also have the worst experiences in the mundane plane. I would explode, my surroundings would get chaotic, or I would just become suddenly disconnected from it all.

After a while, I was able to connect the dots. I remembered the pendulum effect explained in Mickey Singer's book, *The Surrender Experiment*. I could recognize that effect taking place in my life. When I reached the highest connection with the Divine, I inevitably swung back to the other extreme to a worldly disconnection with it all. Then, I continued swinging from side to side until reaching idleness.

What I found different from Mickey's theory was that, after my life swayed like a pendulum reaching the point of balance and idleness, I did not return to the same level of consciousness. I always jumped to a higher level, managing to see life from a higher perspective.

Today my pendulum effects are not as explosive as the previous ones. As soon as I recognize that I am experiencing one of them, I no longer stress. I just relax, because I know the connection will return along with another perspective of life and a higher level of consciousness.

∼

Journal entry October 17, 2017: I have been waking up at four a.m. since initiation day with Yogananda's face in my mind, so excited and energized by him that I begin to meditate right away. The practice of Kriya Yoga includes so many details that I still don't know if I'm doing things right, but I'll continue anyway. I meditate, asking for a strong will to continue.

Journal entry October 19, 2017: Today's meditation was long. I let myself go, and I realized that I don't have to wait for something big to happen. I have to experience and enjoy each meditation because each one will give me something different, something unique. I have the feeling that each meditation is slowly contributing to my progress on this path. What I love the most is that no matter how the meditation turns out to be, once I finish, I always feel very calm and renewed.

Stopping Eating Animal Meat

This process began unconsciously on November 5, 2017, when Joe and I went to an Argentinian steakhouse in Miami, where I tasted the most delicious meat I've eaten, so delicious and tender that we both devoured it in no time.

On our way back home, lethargy fell upon us. We both had the sensation of feeling incredibly full, even though we hadn't eaten much. Fortunately, Troy was staying with his father throughout the weekend, and it was a Sunday afternoon, so the idea of a little nap didn't sound so delusional.

As soon as I got out of the car upon arriving home, I felt as if my body had become extremely heavy. By then, the lethargic state had taken over me completely, so I could barely control my body.

Once home, I climbed what felt like a hundred steps to reach our room on the second floor and dragged myself onto the bed, with shoes and all. While resting there with my eyes lost on the ceiling, I could feel how difficult it was for my organs to process the meat I had recently devoured. That heavy digestion had been the cause for all of my body's other functions to slow down, causing the lethargic state I was in. With that last thought in my mind, I dozed off.

When I finally regained consciousness, it was already dark. I had a terrible taste in my mouth that had forced me out of my sleep. At that moment, I began to carefully consider whether I needed to move since each attempt intensified an unbearable headache. What the hell was wrong with me? I tried to remember without forcing my brain too much. I felt like I was experiencing the worst hangover in history, but I only had one glass of wine, while Joe had none, and he was still sleeping. What was happening to us?

Then I felt it again, that terrible taste in my mouth. This time, I tried harder to discover what it was, and as soon as I realized it, I began to feel nauseous. It was the taste of blood from the meat! I got up running from the bed towards the bathroom, thinking that I was going to let it all out, but this didn't happen. Instead, I went to the sink and started to desperately brush my teeth, as if by doing this, everything would return to normal.

While standing in front of the mirror, noticing that I was still fully dressed, I continued thinking, "What the hell happened?" The headache became so intense that it kept me from thinking. So, I took some pain-killer pills, undressed, and went back to bed, assuring myself that I would figure everything out the next day.

When morning came, the opposite happened. I didn't care much about the episode. I just thought, "those Argentinians prepared some wicked meat," and I continued with my day, not caring that I had just slept seventeen hours straight. Although I was not aware of it, that was the first time I had a genuine connection with my body, a link that from that day began to lead me quietly toward a healthier path.

In the following days, a sudden interest in healthier ways of eating took over me, and I started following several healthy food accounts on Instagram. I never wondered where that sudden interest came from. I always supposed it was a normal curiosity to learn about new recipes.

Before I continue, there is something I must clarify. I was raised believing that it wasn't a meal if it didn't include animal protein, so I ate meat for lunch and dinner most days. Not only did I eat animals every single day, but I was also eating fast food three to four days a week.

I only ate healthy when I got pregnant, and that diet only lasted until Troy was about six years old and he began to believe that the only food he liked to eat was hot dogs, pizza, pasta, and chicken nuggets. At that moment, I stopped all my efforts and returned to Pizza Hut, Shake Shack, Taco Bell, and KFC while making Troy his four favorite dishes and a couple of healthy options that I forced him to eat.

Fortunately, I had inherited my mother's genes, and my weight had always been around 117 pounds regardless of my terrible nutrition. But when I started working from home and became more sedentary, my mother's genes decided to bail on me, and so my weight problems began.

When I realized that my mom's genes had left never to come back, I was thirty-five years old and on vacation with my family in Spain. I remember that while walking down one of the streets, I noticed through my reflection in a store window that the back of my legs looked like cottage cheese. I asked my sister if what I was seeing was correct, and she confirmed it. I desperately ran into the first pharmacy I could find to check my weight. I was 137 pounds. I had gained more than twenty pounds over my average weight, and I hadn't even realized it. I couldn't blame it on Troy because he was already five years old. The worst thing was that I was in Madrid, one of the cities with the most delicious food, and a place that I visit mostly to eat, so that trip became a nightmare.

After that vacation, I needed a plan to return to my normal weight. Since I thought that I was smarter than nature, I believed that I either needed to start eating less or workout more.

I didn't want to make any changes to my diet. So I continued to eat terribly and began to work out. Eating whatever I wanted was a pleasure for me. When I indulged in a food that I craved, I forgot about everything else. Eating had become my way of releasing anxiety rather than fueling my body. Food had become a kind of drug for me.

Every time I sat down to eat, the world around me disappeared. I became a beast devouring whatever was put in front of it. The only way I stopped eating was when I felt totally full and about to explode, and gradually, I was able to eat more and more, a situation that could go on forever.

After exercising for a while, I noticed that my body had not improved; the exercise only prevented me from gaining weight. I realized that I had to start controlling what I was eating, and so my next great idea arrived.

This time, I decided to eat less and continue exercising. Eating less was a nightmare that created so much anxiety that prevented me from losing weight instantly. I spent more than a year on a diet while exercising four times a week to lose those twenty pounds, and each one of those 365 days was torture. I thought about food all the time, and most of those thoughts were related to the food I couldn't eat, so towards the end, it became almost unbearable.

Only after that nightmare did I begin to think that living on a diet was not the way to live. What I needed to do was to change my whole lifestyle for a healthier one, but I didn't know where or how to start. (This was around the time of my trip to California when I read *Autobiography of a Yogi*.)

At the beginning of this path of enlightenment. I didn't even think about changing my eating habits. In my regard, the people who changed the way they ate while on this path were extremists or people who had been brainwashed. Moreover, the books I was reading at the time about higher consciousness didn't touch upon the subject of food, so I didn't feel that changing my diet was even on the table. I blindly believed that nothing in the world could change the way I had been eating for the past thirty-seven years.

I could never see a connection between the food I ate and the spiritual path I was on. At that time, I believed I was formed of three separate entities: the body, the spirit, and the mind. I believed that I had to work on each one individually to move forward in life. For me, my body was simply a vessel with nothing to do with the driver beyond mere transportation. I would have never believed that what is contained in the food I ate had the power to ground me, elevate me, or simply keep me attached to this mundane world.

I would have never imagined that one day, I would think of myself as one of those cavemen I described at the beginning of the book, oblivious to a bigger reality where our bodies, minds, and spirits are not only connected but are actually one, just like the sea where the water, consciousness, and energy are indistinguishable, being and existing as one.

It took me several months to realize that the more I meditated, the more I was able to feel that unity. As a response, I started to feel my body's reaction to the food, weather, exercises, and hormonal changes.

If I go back to that day in the Argentinian steakhouse, I can see how this connection had started to surface within me, and how I unconsciously started to search for other ways of nourishing my body, stumbling across Rawvana, who at the time was a vegan influencer on Instagram.

When I saw Rawana's Instagram account, my first thought was, Wow, veganism is something that I would never be able to endure, and I was 100 percent sure of it. When I saw her posts, I thought, So, what does she eat? And that must taste terrible. I didn't feel inclined to try it, but I wanted to know more about it, so I dove into her YouTube channel.

Rawvana had just released her first book; the fact that it was electronic made it so convenient that I bought it and downloaded it immediately. It took only one hour to read, and I found it very inspiring and straightforward. I quickly became more interested in this new world.

I was intrigued by a specific part of the book, where Rawvana describes how she felt lighter and more linked to Earth while being a raw vegan. This statement got me hooked. Before, I used to be very skeptical about people's recommendations. But after my experience with Kriya Yoga, I started to believe that there are books out there that would speak truth to you. I was already trying this method of enlightenment, and it was working its magic on me. What if another type of nutrition could speed up my enlightenment process?

The book suggested a three-day juice cleanse. The way she described its benefits spoke to me, making me think that it was possible. It wasn't that I believed 100 percent that I could do it, but it opened the door to the possibility. Filled with inspiration, I ordered the food, and I was ready and eager to start.

The plan was to begin with a three-day juice cleanse, then eat raw vegan for a week. After that, I wanted to commit to eating vegan, vegetarian, and pescatarian, each one of them for as long as I could. My main goal was to test them all and feel the differences within me. I wanted to explore how my body and mind reacted to each type of nutrition to decide what to do next.

What worried me the most was the three-day juice cleanse. I had never skipped breakfast, lunch, or dinner. And I didn't think my body could be tricked into believing that a smoothie was an actual meal. Whenever I hadn't had anything to eat before 10 a.m., my blood pressure started to drop, and I would quickly lose consciousness. But I was determined to give this a try, and I was fully aware that I was doing it under my responsibility. I was sure that if I didn't feel like I could continue, I would just quit. Finally, the food arrived, and I was ready to begin my journey.

Journal entry November 15, 2017: My morning meditation was terrific. Today is the first day of my detox with juices, and I feel amazing. It is exactly how Rawvana described it: I feel super light. At the same time, I think that if I achieve this, I can accomplish anything, and that inspires me to continue every time my stomach growls at me. It's a little tricky when I have to prepare dinner for Troy and Joe, but every time I feel I could fail, I realize that I am one step closer to my goal.

Journal entry November 17, 2017: Yesterday was the second day of my cleanse. My brain feels very clear. I can't deny that I'm a bit irritable, but I haven't had a headache. I do feel physically weak, so I try not to do anything exhausting, but I have lots of energy inside, which is very strange. This had never happened to me. It all comes from within.

Today is the last day, and I think I will make it. There are two more hours left in my day, so I will drink the juice and go to bed. There are some things in life that you have always thought you weren't capable of, or maybe that you would never do because they sounded too crazy. Well, here I am, finishing a three-day cleanse with nothing but juice. Yes, I miss chewing, but this is an experience like no other, something that has to be lived and experienced at least once. I am sure that I will do it again because, without a doubt, this has been the most beautiful and intense body experience I have ever had.

Journal entry November 18, 2017: Well, I made it. I finished my cleanse without cheating! When I woke up this morning, I went to the refrigerator and grabbed a tomato, which was the first thing I found, and as soon as I took the first bite, an explosion of flavors brought my taste buds to life.

I could not believe that I had never realized this before. A tomato doesn't taste like a plain tomato! It is a combination of flavors that give that result. I continued to slowly savor that tomato as if it was the most delicious and exotic fruit I had ever tasted. With each bite, I tried diligently to identify every flavor in it. This realization meant that every time I had eaten some fruit or vegetable in the past, what I tasted wasn't a single flavor; instead, it was a combination that produced that specific taste. It was as if nature had already cooked for us, mixing the ingredients until the final product was formed.

Journal entry November 19, 2017: I just finished my meditation, and I feel very peaceful and replenished. Being on this path has aroused this curiosity within me to try new things, and that is the only reason I am trying different ways to nourish my body. I am not doing it because I am following someone or because yogis do it. For me, this is another experiment, similar to the one I am doing with the scientific method of enlightenment. I want to try it and see how each type of nutrition works and feels within me.

Today I am trying to run away from labels experiencing as much as I can. If I have found this treasure of Kriya Yoga and these different nutritional approaches that make me feel things that I have never experienced before, I can't imagine how many other treasures are out there waiting to be found.

This weekend we watched the movie *Cowspiracy*, and it made me think that the body knows exactly what it needs to thrive, and, according to that, it sends us the signs to make us feel like eating a specific food. I was able to experience something similar to this during my pregnancy; my cravings were particular foods that contained nutrients that I was not getting enough of. I feel that our connection with our body is there, but somehow it has been distorted because if I listen to my body right now, it will definitely ask me for a cake with lots of frosting. I have to be patient, and maybe one day, I will hear my body's true voice.

I have noticed how the cleanse with juice has rebooted my body: my urine is now translucent, my body is discharging every day, whereas before, I suffered from constipation. My taste buds have changed completely, allowing me to savor the complexity in every flavor. I also noticed that I used to eat very salty or very sweet; now, I can't stand too much salt or sugar. I think it's still too early to decide if I can live with a vegan or even a raw vegan diet. I don't want to put a label on the way I eat. Nobody knows my body better than my body itself, so I'll quiet all the fuss around me and try to listen to it.

The time had come to start eating raw vegan. After having my raw breakfast with fruits in the morning, I was so caught up with work that lunchtime passed by without me even noticing it. Later in the afternoon, I became so hungry that I caved in. My mind started to point out all the reasons why I needed to eat "real food."

I left home, running to a nearby restaurant. By then, my mind had already selected the target: a chicken and brie cheese sandwich I was addicted to. I was salivating the whole five minutes it took me to get there. I could smell it and feel its taste in my mouth since I left home. If only that would have been enough.

This episode wasn't like the one with the tomato yesterday. This time, I felt like a lion, and the sandwich was my prey. Once I had it in front of me, I swallowed the whole thing in two bites; then, I drank some water desperately as if that liquid would clean my system from any evidence of what I had just done.

I left the place and quickly returned home. I don't think I have to elaborate on how I felt the rest of the afternoon. Morally, I was devastated. I couldn't believe that I had caved in. I was doing so well. My body did not react well to the atomic bomb that I sent right down my throat. I felt heavy and lethargic, so I couldn't eat or do much the rest of the day until an hour ago when I started with a late-night meditation and finished this addition to the journal.

The next day, I resumed the plan. I didn't want to let that failure ruin my entire program. I committed to eating raw vegan for a week, which I carried out without any setback. Then, I started with my vegan diet, which I would continue for as long as I could.

At the beginning of this culinary adventure, I was so excited that I didn't realize how close we were to the end of the year and its holiday celebrations. It is a tradition in my family to get together at the beginning of December for an entire day to prepare a special Venezuelan dish that we eat during the rest of the month. My mom, who was in town visiting us for Christmas, was adamant about following the tradition. Hallacas is the name of the meal and includes beef, pork, and chicken.

When I tried to persuade my mom that I wasn't going to be part of that tradition this year because I was not eating chicken, meat, pork, eggs, or milk, she looked at me dumbfounded and asked, "So, what do you eat?" The situation reminded me of when I asked the same question the first time I saw Rawvana's posts on Instagram. I told her that I ate everything else, to which she replied, "Like what?" I quickly realized that I was not going to win that battle, so I finally accepted that I would spend the whole day preparing Hallacas.

Christmas arrived, and I was still in my vegan phase. As it was too much pressure to sit down at the table with all the food that I had been eating since I was a child without being able to eat it, I made my second exception on my nutritional journey.

For New Year's Eve of 2017, I had invited friends and family home to celebrate. They were all meat-eaters, but some didn't eat pork, so I had to prepare a special dish for them. For some crazy reason, I decided to cook a duck. I had never cooked a duck in my life, but my sister-in-law had done it for Thanksgiving and told me it was easy to prepare. At that point, I thought that if I dared to eat it, I better have the courage to cook it.

I had a lot of experience cooking chicken, but it had always been segmented, boneless, and skinless, making it harder to see what I was actually preparing. Although I tried to postpone buying the duck to see if, miraculously, something happened that would free me from my dilemma, I found myself running to the store at the last minute to buy the frozen death animal.

The preparation seemed fairly easy since everything was already done. I just needed to stuff it and put it in the oven. What could go wrong? Right? Well, when I was trying to put the stuffing inside, I noticed that there was something else inside the thawed animal, when I pulled it out and looked at it, I realized that it was a mesh bag containing the heart along with other small organs of the poor little duck. As soon as I understood what I was holding, I threw it in the trash, quickly washed my hands, and carried my gagging body all the way to the bathroom. Once there, I finally knelt before the toilet, letting everything out.

After that, I couldn't find the strength or morale to come back and finish cooking. I sat on the bathroom floor, arguing with myself as to why I was doing that. Why hadn't I bought the duck already made? It was getting late, and I needed to start cooking if I wanted my friends to eat something more than salad at dinner.

While still on the bathroom floor, I tried to remember if I had ever felt that eating animal meat was wrong and so I traveled through my memories to a day in my childhood. We were in the countryside, visiting relatives in my mother's hometown. The whole family was gathered in the backyard. It was the first time I visited that house. I spent the entire morning excited, running after the hens, roosters, and little chicks that roamed freely in the yard while the adults talked and laughed. I remember that when lunchtime arrived, nobody seemed to be preparing any food in the kitchen. So, I started looking for my *Abuela* (grandmother) everywhere, and when I finally found her, I asked her what was for lunch.

She was heading towards the courtyard but turned back to look at me and replied: "Chicken!!"with a grin on her face. I continue to follow her totally clueless about what was to come. Once outside, she glanced at the innocent birds, asking me, "Which one do you like?" I remember looking around at all the sweet creatures I was playing with a few minutes ago. I didn't know if what I was hearing was real, so I decided to think it was just a joke until my grandmother started walking towards one of the white hens. She grabbed the hen by the head and trapped its body under her arm, to suddenly pull the head off the neck.

All of this was happening while the adults were looking at me laughing as if it was entertaining for them to see my reaction to that barbaric scene. I was about seven or eight years old, but even at that young age, I felt that what I had witnessed wasn't right. So, why were the adults doing it and thinking it was even funny?

When I returned from that memory, I was still sitting on the bathroom floor. My stomach was a terrible mess, and I had no idea what to do with the duck I had waiting for me in the kitchen. Eventually, I got the courage to get up from the floor and return to the kitchen to finish what I had begun.

I can't deny that I felt terrible throughout the entire process. I still have the image of the poor duck in what looked like a fetal position tattooed on the back of my mind. I did what I had to do and quickly placed the duck in the oven. My stomach was so disturbed that I couldn't eat anything that New Year's Eve. However, I drank everything I could get my hands on, with the hopes that my inebriated mind could forget about that terrible experience.

The next day, it was January first, and I began to eat vegetarian for a month. Immediately afterward, I ate pescatarian for the next three months. By then, I believed that my goal was accomplished. I had learned a lot during those six months, but I never considered myself vegan, vegetarian, or pescatarian. Thus, the day arrived for me to decide how I was going to nourish my body from that day on.

I used the last month of that culinary journey to decide what to do after my experiment and I came to the conclusion that I wanted to continue listening to my body regarding its nutrition and its needs. I wanted to quit following labels. My connection with my body was not that strong yet, but I knew it was there. I just needed to work on it. I needed to stop listening to what everyone around me said and listen within me, and if I didn't receive an answer, I just had to try again and again. I didn't worry about making mistakes while developing that connection, because, at the end of the day, they would be my own mistakes, not the mistakes of others. I felt very motivated, but

I wanted to give myself time to embrace this process without judging it.

Ever since the duck episode, I haven't eaten poultry, and I think I never will again. As for red meat, I must confess that I ate it about four times after finishing that culinary journey. And I could lie to you by saying that in those opportunities, I was so hungry that I couldn't think clearly, or that I was being polite with family or friends when they offered me some. But to be fully honest, I must admit that I wanted to eat red meat, and not only those times, but every time that after an enormous effort on my part, I had decided not to. Listening to my body caused me a lot of turmoil even when I didn't eat red meat, as I feel like a hypocrite because I knew I wanted to eat it.

Those were blurry days, as in any growth process. Only when I quieted my mind, I was able to feel that my body didn't need any meat. I could even feel its repulsion to it. Nonetheless, on those weak days when my mind became restless, and my senses ran wild and untamed, the urgency and the craving returned. I knew the situation was not sustainable and that, sooner than later, I would cave in.

That prediction materialized on a November day in 2018, about a year after my experience in the Argentinian steak-house that had started me on this culinary path. Early on that day, I began to feel an insane urge to eat meat, which didn't let me think about anything else. It had been more than four months since the last time I had eaten red meat. Curiously, when the urge arrived, I was not hungry at all. I only felt an inexplicable craving, which I fought and overcame, as usual. I tried not to make a big deal about it, but the same thought appeared again shortly after. I knew that if it wasn't that day, I would soon give up.

This second time, I started to doubt; what if this urge is my body telling me it needs the freaking meat.?? Confused by the whole situation, I decided to eat the meat for which I salivated desperately. However, this time after considering the intensity of the craving, I promised myself that if after eating it, I wanted to reintegrate it into my diet, I would do it without hesitation.

That night, we went to the same Argentinian restaurant. The meat was as delicious as the first time. Soon after we finished eating, I asked myself if that meant that I would go back to eating meat again. To my surprise, my reply was a harsh, "No." I was completely petrified. How could I, after eating the meat I had been craving for so many months, decide that I didn't want to eat it ever again? I waited to get home so I could ponder about what was going on within me.

Once home, I wasn't able to find any answers, so I let it sit for a while. Frankly, I thought that sooner or later, I would want to eat meat again. Yet, I wanted to wait until the last revision of this book to see what happened after that November day.

To my amazement, I didn't feel the need to eat meat or even fish. On Christmas that year, I made vegan hallacas and felt very true to myself. I had also been to Shake Shack, a place I'd die for in the past, and just sat there without eating while a friend devoured everything on the table. The hamburgers that once melted in my mouth had become anything but food to me.

Although I was relieved, I wondered why I wasn't eating any meat: no poultry, no fish, or red meat. Why was the craving gone? Why didn't I do it if I had allowed myself to eat it all again?

Deep down, I knew the reason, but I felt too ashamed to admit it because the person I used to be would usually challenge and mock people who thought the way I was now thinking.

The reality was that I didn't eat it because I felt it wasn't necessary to kill an animal to feed myself. The remorse over eating an animal was more significant than the fleeting satisfaction of my palate. If there were so many food options, why would I prefer to eat a dead animal? And not only that, over time, I had noticed that my body thrived more when I nourished it with foods that were alive like plants and fruits. I felt as if the energy contained in them blended with mine once inside me, while dead animals made me feel the opposite of that.

Once I was honest with myself, I got more clarity about me, about who I was and where I was going. Honestly, I don't know how that understanding arose in me. I suppose that it was another one of those magical moments of realization that have been occurring along this path. Suddenly, something clicked inside me, and I could no longer see animal meat as food.

This nutrition journey taught me many things, but one of the most important was not related to food. It was the importance of not judging or putting pressure on others regarding what they eat. Today I feel unable to criticize others for doing something I did for thirty-eight years. I understand that everyone is on their own path. I have also abandoned the belief that something is good or bad, right or wrong.

Today, when people ask me if I am vegan or vegetarian, my answer is: "Sometimes," and I wait for the laughs at the absurdity of my response to avoid the subject altogether. I don't feel like explaining what I don't eat and why I don't eat it. What I eat now is not related to what is trendy or what others are eating. No, what I eat today is far from that; it comes from this trial and error effort, from my attempt to connect with my body and whatever it needs to thrive.

Nutrition for me has become a sacred experience far from what it was in those Taco Bell days. Sacred because, if you look at it closely, it's not just about the food you eat. It's way more than that. It's also the time and the love that you pour into each meal: from its purchase, its preparation, until that instant when you are finally at the table, tasting each bite.

Sometimes I get so ruffled, thinking that there are more important things to do, and in that rush, the essential things in life like nourishment shrink to nothing. Then, one morning, while eating something as simple as overnight oats with banana and cinnamon, I can perceive that connection again. During those minutes, I can feel my body thanking me in every spoonful that goes between my lips, and with the sweetness of that moment, I connect with all that is truly important again.

Raising Our Children

I have decided to leave my son, Troy, largely out of this book for respect to his privacy. I am the one who has chosen to open up and showcase my life for everyone to see. Nonetheless, I have included these lines to share with you how this awakening process has affected my life as a mother.

I used to believe that being a mother was the best feeling in the world, but I never had any idea if I was doing it right. Being an awakened mother has given me a sense of understanding and clarity that I never had before. It had helped me to establish a connection with Troy that it would not have been possible to achieve otherwise.

This connection seems to come from an unknown world, but it is here between us; I feel it every time he looks at me. It's a union that gently teaches me how to guide him and how to let myself be guided by him.

When I see him, I see that purity of consciousness that I work relentlessly to go back to.

Before, I had the concept of motherhood totally wrong. I thought that I was here to teach him, but how could I have taught him anything in those days when I had no idea who I was or what I was doing with my life? How could I have taught him anything if I was just winging it through life? How could I even explain to him some of the rules of a society that seem ridiculous to me, and from which I am trying to run away?

Sadly, during all those years of motherhood, I had forced him to see life through my perspective, inheriting my fears and limitations instead of allowing him to develop his own view of the world.

I am not saying that today, after following this path, I am a perfect mom, not at all. There are still times where I find myself quite lost and absorbed again in those archaic methods to raise our children. In those moments, I confuse my guidance with authority, with ego, or with any other of those biases, and I explode, scream, and complain—but surely way less than before.

The only difference is that today, I have this inexplicable certainty that I am on the right track and that I am putting in my honest effort. So when those blurry days try to take over, I have the wisdom to consciously and quickly come back to center.

Why Don't We Treat Ourselves the Way We Treat Our Children?

Journal entry November 25, 2017: Today was one of those days when you make a wish and receive it instantly. Even as I write these lines, I can still feel the echoes of that fulfilled yearning. At first, I didn't have any expectations. I just felt like asking for it with the hope that someday I might receive it. But today, I immediately received it.

It all started this morning when I began my meditation. I bowed to the masters and asked them to please give me the clarity of mind that I felt I needed to perceive the Divine. When my first present arrived, I perceived a delicate fragrance that I had never been in contact with before. On my next inhalation, I tried to confirm if what I have smelled was real and there it was, offering itself to me again. The fragrance was so delicate and so exquisite that I didn't want to mess things up by asking questions, so I just accepted what had just happened.

Then, as I continued with the meditation, I felt a numbing sensation in my arms that prevented me from moving my hands. Within a few seconds, the numbing had expanded throughout my entire body. I wanted to experience what was happening without being judgmental. I wasn't interested in any absurd description that my mind could give to what was happening to me.

I asked for my mind to stop thinking, and when that wish was suddenly granted, I found myself floating peacefully. After a long time in that state, I realized that I was able to move my arms again, and, little by little, my whole body was returned to me. I thanked my masters for such beautiful presents, and I realized that an entire hour had passed.

Previously, I saw these experiences only as gifts; now I also see them as a confirmation that I am on the right path. I see them as clues to keep going.

The rest of the day, I kept on thinking about the dear friend I had lunch with on Sunday. There was something about that encounter that disturbed me greatly because while my friend was talking about one of her problems, I could hear and feel in her voice how harsh and strict she was with herself. Although I told her several times that she shouldn't worry so much or be so severe, my words couldn't reach her. It was as if I thought I was talking, but there wasn't any sound coming out of my mouth.

Her problems were like many of mine, such as not knowing what to do next with her life, or feeling trapped doing something that didn't inspire her. I knew she should be more kind, loving, tender, and forgiving to herself, and at this time, I had a revelation. Was I sweet, loving, tender, and forgiving with myself? I had to reply with a firm, "No, I am not!" So, if I am not able to feel this way for myself, why do I think it would be easy for others to do so?

I allowed myself to go a little further. If I was not tender and loving with myself, how could I be that way with Troy, Joe, or with this dear friend? Why do I always have to demand more and more from myself without showing any compassion or love? Or why don't I at least recognize the times when I am giving the best of me?

At that moment, I felt like a little girl, and I began to think about all the immense love I feel for Troy. Why haven't we learned that we must not only love our children in this way? Why haven't we learned to love ourselves this way?

When Troy tells me that he is not feeling well, I listen to him. I tell him to go and rest. I prepare his favorite food, take it to his bed, and stay by his side. I let him watch his favorite shows on my computer and spoil him rotten until he feels better. Why don't I listen to myself when I am tired or not feeling well?

When he tries his best and fails, I have compassion for him, comfort him, and help him forget the incident, reminding him that nothing, nothing in the world, is that important to make him feel so bad. Why, when this happens to me, do I treat myself like a loser?

I had no responses to this. I couldn't understand why I did not treat myself as I treated the people I love the most, and I couldn't justify my behavior. Maybe I have been missing that self-love that everybody talks about...It's getting late, and it has been an intense day. I will just let this discovery sink in, and maybe further along on my path, I will be able to see the answer.

After that day, I have been more compassionate towards myself, I have consciously started to treat myself as I would treat Troy, and this has tremendously impacted my life. I feel that little by little, this has filled me with a love for myself so tender that I couldn't compare it with anything other than the love of a mother. It was so evident that this love was not there before, but I needed to realize it within me. I had to wait for that magical instant of realization to change the way I treated myself.

Pablo Alborán

Journal entry October 5, 2017: Since the beginning of this path, I have been receiving presents here and there. Lately, I have come to the realization that some of them are related to people who can create magic. The more I am exposed to these elating instances, the more I get acquainted with the power of creation.

This new present received from the Universe was in the form of an invitation from my best friend, Jenny, to the press release of Pablo Alborán's new album in Miami. Pablo is my favorite Spanish singer and songwriter. He has that special touch similar to Jack Johnson: They both create with their music and their performances a magic so pure, and so unique that it can make your whole being tremble.

Unlike Jack Johnson's concert, this one was very intimate. There were less than fifty people invited. The new album was called *Saturn*, and the presentation was held at the recently opened Miami Planetarium.

From the moment the doors opened, you could undoubtedly feel the magical encounter between a man and his creation. Every detail had been exquisitely thought out.

Right there, in the darkness of that mystical planetarium, we abandoned the earthly and surrendered to a new dimension created by the artist on his Saturn.

I was profoundly moved by the delicacy of this gift. For the first time in my life, I got to feel with my whole being the love of an artist for what he did. While feeling dazzled by the experience, I couldn't stop asking myself, how could someone create such magic?

We were all in the dark, united by that magical thread that bound us to him, and ecstatic by the anticipation of seeing and hearing the person who was able to awaken within us such delightful feelings.

After a few minutes, the anxious waiting was displaced by the first chords of a piano. Each note kept you captive, seduced, lured. From the darkness, the lights began to emerge, revealing the person that fuelled all these emotions. He was there, sitting at his piano, gently inviting us to travel with each word, to a moment in our life similar to the one coming out from his lips.

While watching and enjoying that scene with my whole being, I began to look for a word that could sum up what I had been experiencing since I entered that place. It wasn't until the end of the song when the term was revealed to me: inspiration. Yes, inspiration was the word that embraced that universal and elevated power that helps us to create magic.

During those hours, I couldn't decipher why the Universe had invited me to be part of all that. It wasn't until later on this journey when I managed to see how that inspiration that I experienced between Pablo and his Saturn silently guided me to meet face to face with mine...with my inspiration, with my creation, with my Saturn.

9

FEELING GUIDED: THE IDEA OF WRITING A BOOK IS BORN

Journal Entry November 27, 2017: Today I am overwhelmed with happiness. During meditation this morning, I was able to feel for a few minutes the second divine quality that Kriya Yoga offers to its practitioners: the divine light. I was supposed to have experienced this light during my initiation. Still, I didn't, and I had totally forgotten about it until today, so it was a pleasant and beautiful surprise. The feeling was very timid at first but intensified as the seconds passed.

I had many other magical experiences this weekend. One of them was being able to feel once again the pure love that exists within me. This time, I did not experience it as intensely as when my niece Annabelle was born. Instead, this delightful love manifested itself as a feeling of peace and abundance that made my whole body beam with pure bliss, granting me a sense of connectedness with it all.

Another amazing experience that I had this Sunday occurred on my way to the KYIO ashram in Homestead. My previous week had been a bit intense workwise, causing some disturbance on my emotional balance, which made me easily irritable. So when Sunday finally arrived, I needed the peace of the ashram to comfort me.

Most of the time, when I go there, I sit and meditate with the group. Once the meditation session is over, I stay lying down a few more minutes, savoring the sweet post-meditation elixir that always lingers. Other times, I wander around the ashram grounds surrounding myself with the lush vegetation, filled with so much beauty; I indulge listening to nothingness.

When lunchtime arrives, I sit in silence with the rest of the practitioners. We eat slowly and smile at each other with delightful complicity, and even without saying a word for those four hours, I feel such an intense cleanse within that always keeps me coming back for more.

So, this Sunday, I was missing the whole experience.

Troy was with his dad the entire weekend; thus, as soon as I finished my breakfast, I got in my car and started driving to the ashram. I had precisely forty-five minutes to get there, which was what it usually took me. I had been there about three times so far since my initiation, and I had always used the GPS as I was not familiar with the area, and many of the streets were often closed by construction work.

With the craziness of the week, I had forgotten to pay my cell phone bill, but I only noticed that my phone was disconnected when I was already fifteen minutes away from home. If I went back to pay the bill, I wouldn't make it in time for the meditation. On the other hand, I had no idea how to get to this place, so sadly, I decided to go back home and forget about the group meditation.

When I was looking for the next exit, a voice within told me, "I will guide you." The message was so bizarre that while I was trying to figure out where it was coming from, I missed the exit. Hearing that voice made me realize that I didn't have anything to lose. Besides, I really wanted to go to the ashram, so I decided I would let myself be guided.

I knew how to get to Homestead, but I didn't know the ashram's exact address. While driving, I tried in vain to remember the road I had taken and the turns I had made to get there in the past, but nothing came to me; instead, I started to stress out. I was so concentrated on trying to remember the directions that I got off the turnpike and onto US-1 by mistake, thereby making the drive even longer.

I decided to calm down, thinking that if something within me was telling me that it would guide me, I should believe in it. But... Did I believe in it? The answer was, not really. I considered it highly unlikely that I would be guided to the ashram without any delay. The funny thing was that although I believed it was unlikely, I kept on driving; I guess deep down, I wanted to know if it was possible and if that voice spoke the truth.

So, while I was driving, with no phone, no GPS, no help, and alone, I felt a similarity between that situation and all the times I have arrived at crossroads in my life where I had no idea which direction to take. In these kinds of situations, I had always made a rush decision instead of waiting for the sign or the right moment. So this time, I decided to continue to let myself be guided and wait for that hint.

I knew the ashram was somewhere on the right side of the road but filled with doubts, I wanted to turn at every traffic light. All the corners looked familiar to me. While I was lost in my internal battle, the same voice interrupted me, saying, "I will let you know when to turn," and I just continued while thinking that none of that made any sense. I might be able to find the place if I had more time, but the whole point was to arrive in time for group meditation. I didn't want to get lost and wait another week.

I hushed myself and tried to think about the address, but I couldn't remember it exactly. I believed the place was somewhere around 267 Street, and I was at 247 Street. So, I continued driving.

The next traffic light was a big intersection. The red light left me waiting, and while I waited, I couldn't stop looking to the right side of the road, trying hard to find something that seemed familiar to me, but I couldn't find anything. With disappointment, I began to anticipate the next intersection. I looked then to the left to release the tension in my neck caused by staring to the right for so long.

As soon as I looked to the left and allowed myself to relax for a few seconds, the building on the corner immediately caught my attention. It was a large restaurant painted in white with blue doors and windows, which seemed very familiar to me.

By then, the light had changed to green, and the cars in the first row had begun to move forward. I pressed on the clutch, to be ready when my turn came. Although my attention was still drawn to the building, I noticed out of the corner of my eye that the car in front of me was advancing.

I looked forward and was ready to change the gear and speed up, but in that second, I remembered that a few weeks ago, Joe and Troy had driven me to the ashram. We had stopped at the same intersection, but we were at the traffic light next to that restaurant. We were coming from the road that was now on my left as we had just come off the turnpike. That day, I had looked through the window, and the same restaurant had caught my attention since there aren't many buildings in that part of town, and one painted white and blue was difficult to miss.

I remember trying to figure out how a Greek restaurant could survive in the countryside, but as we started to move forward, I read the name and realized that it was actually a Mexican restaurant called Puerto Vallarta. Yes! It was the same one!! That was my sign!! The cars behind me were already honking their horns, so I quickly put my indicator, sped up, changed lanes, and finally turned right.

I was in disbelief, not only because I had received the sign but also because it seemed so bizarre that all this was actually happening. I would have never chosen to come throughout US-1 and to be stopped by a red light long enough to have the time to look to the left and be able to find that same restaurant seemed unreal to me.

As I advanced down that road, everything suddenly became familiar: the house with the fancy fence, the nursery on the corner, the smoothie place on the right. I knew I was on the right path, although I still didn't know when to make the next turn, or if I needed to turn left or right. I was deep in the countryside, but when I felt like I was going to freak out again, I remembered what had just happened. I had received this incredible demonstration that I was being guided, and if all that had happened, anything else could be possible. I decided to relax and continue driving. There were no more voices to be heard, but this time I had the certainty that I was going to make it.

After more than ten minutes, I recognized a school and a business, so I knew I was still on the correct path. I continued for another five minutes, and when I stopped at the next intersection, I looked around, and I was able to recognize the trees that surrounded the ashram. I turned right, and as simple as that I was greeted by the pebbled road that had welcomed me several times already.

How improbable was all of it—I was there, on time, without a single wrong turn. What if life was as simple as that, and we were the ones who complicated it? What if we just needed to relax, trust, and wait until we feel this certainty within? What if we only need to stop this rattling within that makes us choose whatever option is immediately available, and instead become calm and attentive, patiently waiting until we feel from within that we have found the sign, and that the time has come?

I was lost in those thoughts as I walked towards the building. I had no time to spare. I passed through the rose circle next to the parking lot and went inside to begin the group meditation.

The meditation was sweet and delicate. I lay down for a few minutes after finishing, delighted by the after-meditation feeling I was longing for so long. After a while, the bell rang, announcing that lunch was ready, and we all gathered at the wrap-around porch. I felt like I was floating through it all. I sat on the floor and smiled at my neighbors.

The girl sitting on my right was so radiant that I was able to feel her energy. I usually eat in silence to slowly savor the delicious food that our dear volunteers prepare. But this time, it was evident that this girl couldn't contain herself and wanted desperately to engage in conversation, so as soon as I looked up to her, she started talking.

We had been initiated on the same day, and I had seen her a couple of times after that, but we had never had a chance to sit down and talk. I guess the time for us to connect had arrived. She started with the remark that we had been initiated together. I smiled and responded with, "Yes, I remember you." From there, she went straight to the point and asked, "What do you think about Kriya Yoga? Do you practice every day?"

It was impossible for me to explain to her how I felt about Kriya Yoga, and specifically that day, after what had just happened to me on the way there. How could I explain all of that? She would think that I had lost my mind, so I kept it simple. "It has definitely changed my life. I practice every day, once a day," and that was all she needed. From there, she started to tell me her story.

She had bumped into Kriya Yoga by mistake when she was looking for "the regular yoga," as she called it. I knew that she was referring to the asanas, the type of yoga that is most widely known. She was living nearby, so Kriya Yoga International Organization popped up in her Google search.

She told me that while visiting the website, she felt "magically attracted to the practice" because it was exactly what she was looking for. She explained that on that day, she felt as if she had been guided to find Kriya Yoga to help her with several issues that were causing a lot of pain in her life.

She wanted to get divorced for a long time already, but her husband had recently been in a car accident. I did not say a word. How could I? I was so interested in her story that I didn't want to distract her.

She went on to say that the day of the initiation was one of the most beautiful days of her life, one that she will always remember. Soon after, her tone became more of a whisper. She shared that after the initiation, many magical "things" had happened to her. I got closer because I didn't want to lose any of it. For me, that meant that I was not crazy, that these sorts of inexplicable "things" did not only happen to me, and that they were not just typical "things" that my insane mind considered magical. No, she was having similar experiences to mine.

I remember her saying that right after her initiation, she went home and told her husband that she needed him to work with her on their marriage. She had supposedly repeated the same thing to him for the last three years, and he had never been open to it, but that day, he magically agreed. She went on to explain all the changes that their marriage had gone through to allow them to be in a healthier relationship. She was still astonished that this practice had such a strong power to transform her life in only five weeks. Then, she continued to share many other magical moments experienced after the initiation.

Every word that came out of her mouth was soothing all of my worries. I told her that similar inexplicable "things" were also happening to me. I wanted to return the favor because I knew that she was feeling the same way I was feeling. No, we were not crazy...magical things were happening to us, and it was all right...more than all right.

That evening after returning from the ashram, during my practice of Ashtanga Yoga, I noticed that I was starting to surrender more. The teacher was on top of my back, adjusting me while I was in paschimottanasana, exhaling slowly and letting it all go. As I let go, I was able to fold deeper than ever before, and for the first time, I was able to touch my calves with my forehead. There was no pain, only amazement that I could bend that deep, that I was capable of so much without knowing it. Everything seemed extremely beautiful to me; the vibrations, the surrender, feeling the divine within me.

After this magical weekend, and after feeling the divine light this morning during my meditation, I sat down and reflected on the significance of all those moments lived. I remember feeling special when I just realized that I was being guided, thinking that maybe only a few people were able to feel or experience all of this. But then when the girl at the ashram couldn't contain her happiness about everything that was happening to her after Kriya Yoga, I had no doubt that we are all able to experience this awareness, this magic, this bliss, just like her, just like me.

So while I write these lines in my journal, I find myself beaming with the desire to tell everyone about this world that has opened its doors not only to me but to everyone that has the fervent desire to see beyond the mundane. I want to share what I am experiencing with as many people as I can. So after much thought, I've decided to compile all of my journal entries and self-studies in a book that recounts my story and inspires others to seek and follow their path. A path where they can feel all the magic and absolute happiness that today only some of us have been able to enjoy.

10

MY RETREAT AT YOGANANDA'S HERMITAGE

Journal entry March 22, 2018: I am writing these lines before bedtime. Tomorrow I'll fly to San Diego to visit Yogananda's hermitage for the first time. I have never felt this excited about a trip before. I woke up this morning, embraced by a delicate and warm sensation. My heart had somehow opened up, letting go of a pressure I had on my chest, making me weightless, able to float again. I am starting to notice that every time this open heart sensation visits me, everything moves slower, even I move slower as if experiencing life on a deeper level.

I have the impression that some strange forces have brought me here, where I am today, ready for this trip. Everything has happened so fast, and out of nowhere that makes me believe that going to this place is of great importance in my life, but I have no idea why. I guess I will figure it out soon.

I decided to go to this retreat at the ashram of the Self-Realization Fellowship (SRF) in Encinitas, California, just two weeks ago, when Troy's father told me that he wanted to spend spring break with him, and Joe found himself tied up with work. I interpreted all that as a sign to get away and connect with myself on a deeper level, to be alone, accompanied only by my meditation and my writing.

While trying to figure out where to go, I connected instantly to the moment when I received the welcome package from SRF a few months earlier. That package included a booklet with several places where the institution hosted retreats.

When I visited the SRF website, I was immediately attracted to the retreat in Encinitas, California, because I remembered that was the hermitage where Yogananda finished writing his *Autobiography of a Yogi*, the book that changed my life. Yes, that was the place where I wanted to spend that week, totally disconnected from the mundane world, and fully submerged in my own.

I wanted to experience what it meant to be there, feeling Yogananda's energy as I feel Hariharananda's when I go to his Homestead ashram. I immediately contacted the organization, and after a couple of days, they confirmed my stay.

Journal entry March 23, 2018: I am at the Santa Fe Depot train station writing these lines, while I wait for the train that will take me to Encinitas. I find myself savoring every second of this trip. Could the watch move its minute hand any slower so I can prolong this newfound happiness?

Being here in California is unexpected. When we returned from San Diego to Los Angeles eight months ago, I was really sad to leave California, as I found myself quite seduced by the diversity and beauty of the state. I remember thinking that I wouldn't visit the West Coast for a long time since I had nothing to do here, not even friends or family to visit. So when we left, I thought I wouldn't be back in a long time. But, here I am today, sitting at the train station, looking at the beautiful mosaics that dress up the walls of the waiting hall.

I have to confess that I have always been fascinated by trains and their stations, the older, the better. I don't know why, but I find them romantic. They transport me to those golden times when through their corridors and grand doors, thousands of people passed in and out daily. So, whenever I can, I get on one of them and enjoy imagining those days.

It's only five in the afternoon, and I'm really exhausted; all these emotions have depleted my batteries. My train will arrive at any time, and it will take me about an hour to reach the retreat.

Journal entry March 24, 2018: Encinitas is a typical California sea-side town from what I could see walking from the train station yesterday.

The grounds where the compound is seated are quite impressive, not only for their size but also for how well-maintained they are. There are several buildings in the compound, including Yogananda's Hermitage, the retreat, and some offices of the SRF. The property is relatively large and runs along a cliff with indulgent views of beach sunsets along the coast. The retreat is impeccable but still modest and peaceful. The silence gives you the impression that everything moves slower behind its walls, which is a very pleasant sensation.

Yesterday, upon my arrival, I was greeted by one of the ladies in the management office. Everybody here behaves in such a tranquil manner that it unconsciously invites you to act in the same way. She informed me that it was a silent retreat, which I was unaware of until right that second.

Luckily, I had always wanted to do a silent retreat. I have never found silence to be a challenge; I love my moments of solitude and tranquility, and I am definitely not keen on small talk. The fact that the retreat was silent made it even more perfect, as I wouldn't have to socialize with other guests or staff.

The lady accompanied me to my room and explained most of the rules on our way up the stairs. She showed me the place, welcomed me again, and left. I was so exhausted that I took a shower and went straight to bed.

Today I started following the retreat program and woke up at five a.m. to meditate. It wasn't such a problem as I had gone to bed at seven p.m. the night before. The meditation was peaceful and grounding. I had not received the meditation technique from my biweekly lessons from SRF lessons, so I was following the one that I had always practiced from the KYIO.

After my meditation, I took a shower and joined the other attendees downstairs for some exercises. As soon as we finished, the bell rang, indicating that breakfast was served. After eating, we had a group meditation, which I joined as well. This meditation was much harder, maybe because I had never meditated twice in one day with only three hours in between.

Once the meditation finished, I borrowed a book from the library titled *The Journey to Self-Realization* by Yogananda, returned to my room, and started to read. Once I got tired, I began to work on my journal.

Breakfast was a bit amusing this morning when everyone staying at the retreat gathered in the dining room to share their meals. It was a self-service buffet, so talking was not necessary. Nonetheless, it was very obvious that most attendees were struggling with not being allowed to speak.

You could see them desperately trying to express with their faces all of the words they weren't allowed to say, even simple words like hi, thanks, or please. As this happened, I tried to look inward to see if I was affected by any of this so far, but I just felt relieved. I also noticed that not speaking made me more aware of my surroundings and connected with the experience.

Fortunately I was ready to experience it all. Normally I would have freaked out, thinking about what I was going to do in the hours I wasn't eating or meditating. I believed that with this level of excitement, I would probably be sleeping around six hours a day, which meant that I would be awake for more than eighteen without "anything" to do. Instead, the opposite happened.

I surrendered to the experience, and I decided to follow the schedule of the meals, meditations, and group exercises proposed by the retreat, and dedicate the remaining twelve hours to reading and walking. I knew it would be hard to fully disconnect from the mundane world, so I allowed myself to use the Internet for no more than thirty minutes a day.

Detachment of Opinions Self-study

Journal entry March 27, 2018: Last night I went to sleep at six p.m. I still have not adapted to California time. I skipped meditation last night. I was trying to do it in bed, but I ended up falling asleep. I woke up at four a.m., did some work, and tried to do ashtanga yoga in my room. I had a million excuses, so I ended up doing only half of the first series. I continued through my day as usual reading and writing, but by ten a.m., my brain needed a break. I hadn't been online since I arrived, so I got the worst idea. I started to look at my cell phone and went on Instagram.

While going through the publications on my feed, one caught my attention. The post was from someone who has a big name in the yoga (asanas) community. I immediately started to feel an adverse reaction toward this person as I disagreed with every word in the publication.

Blinded by rage, I wanted to comment on it, and for sure, it was not going to be a nice one. Yet when I looked around and realized where I was, I was shocked by the absurdity of it all.

How could I be experiencing such an outburst while I was on a spiritual retreat? Checking Instagram was terrible enough, but my reaction and the idea of writing a negative comment was way too much. I was very disappointed with myself for not taking full advantage of my stay at this place. I was skipping meditations, avoiding yoga, and now on Instagram. What the heck?

Yet, after a few minutes, when my self-preaching ended, and my consciousness quieted down, my mind started to think again about the terrible comment I was going to post. I have never posted a negative comment on social media. I always believed that if someone had taken the time to express their opinion, people who disagree should look the other way, but this time, for some strange reason, I wasn't able to do it. That post had gotten to me; it was moving something within me.

It really didn't matter what the post was about or who posted it. What mattered was the fact that a simple publication had unleashed all this madness inside me.

When I was ready to write the nastiest of comments, my consciousness reappeared out of nowhere, making me analyze the whole situation. How could a simple post catapult me into this rage state? I tried to look inward for this answer. I knew that if I let my mind evaluate the whole situation, I would end up with: Who cares why I react like this? It's simple, this person is wrong and unhinged so I have to express my opinion. Anyway, it's a free country. How can a public person be making statements so far from reality?

Thinking again about the post made me feel even more enraged, so I decided to count to three and go back to my self imposed task of figuring out what was going on with me. At that moment, I asked myself a question that always helped me to put things into perspective. What if the other person is right? As soon as the question popped up in my head, I needed to sit down to cool off. I was so confused. I had so many mixed emotions that I decided to write the way I felt about this subject in my journal. By the time I was done, I was amazed about what came out of my head.

One of my biggest problems today is my opinion. Why do I need to have an opinion about everything? Even if people are not actually asking me for it. If I go on Instagram, I have an opinion on every single post. When I walk on the streets, I have an opinion on every person, every car, every business.

If I go a bit deeper, I am able to notice that my opinions are not the problem. The main issue is my obsessive attachment to them. An opinion is simply a point of view, a perception about something, and I seem to have forgotten to look at it literally. Point of view doesn't mean reality or truth; it merely conveys the perspective we have about something from where we are located at that exact moment.

If I quiet my mind for a few seconds and am honest with myself, I can recognize that I have an obsessive attachment to my opinions. After this realization, I was able to see how my distorted mind had made me believe that my point of view is part of who I am. My opinions have stopped being a mere perception of things or situations to become not only my reality, but the absolute reality, therefore, the only reality that I can see.

The metamorphosis that takes place within me, where due to my obsessive attachment a simple point of view becomes the only reality I can see, keeps me totally blinded. Thus, any opinion that differs from my reality (opinion) becomes, in my eyes, not real, false. That is why when people have opinions that are different from mine, I unconsciously get angry. After all, in my crazy mind, those opinions have nothing to do with "reality," and people who express them are simply "crazy" as they cannot see "the reality."

The most straightforward example to show my craziness, was to remember when years ago a photograph of "the dress" became a viral sensation on the Internet. The dress was actually black and blue, but I saw it white and golden. The strange thing was not that I saw it in a different color, but that I really believed that the dress was white and gold because that was my reality, therefore the only "reality" that existed, and in my absurd mind everyone that saw the dress differently had a visual problem.

I couldn't accept that I was the one with the problem, let alone admit that each person has a very different way of seeing the world, not only caused by eye conditions but also for many other reasons. Perspectives that are neither good nor bad at the end of the day, much less true or false.

If I go back to this morning's episode and analyze it under this new light, I can see that even if the person had posted that he was Superman, this should not affect me. But now, I can see that it affected me because I was unconsciously attached to my point of view in which he was not Superman. I could also see how my opinion was no longer a simple opinion because it had become my reality, "the only reality." Therefore, in my eyes, what was said on the post was completely wrong, and the guy was definitely insane as he was saying something that was not real.

Finally, it is evident that all the anger inside me was not caused by my need to make this guy see how far he was from reality. All the negativity within me was produced because this person was threatening my reality. So, who was crazy here? Who had a problem? I was the crazy one! I had a problem!

The guy who published the post had no problem. He was happy in his reality because he was Superman. What was the solution? The only solution was to accept that I needed to separate myself from my points of view. I had to go back to the elementary school where they teach the literal meaning of point of view to dissuade my mind from the crazy idea of starting World War III with everyone who has a different opinion from mine. And it is as simple as taking a few seconds to remember that my opinion is only a point of view; it is not the absolute reality, much less the absolute truth.

If we look around, most of us are living this way. Most of us are so attached to our opinions that they have become our reality, and our "absolute truth," a truth that some may even kill or die for. It all starts small, so small that we don't even notice it. It could even start with comments full of anger like the one I wanted to post. A publication that creates so much negativity that it unleashes a domino effect into the world and ends up affecting and hurting others. When the truth is that it would only take a second and a lot of courage to realize that our opinions are only our points of view and not the reality, much less the absolute truth ... and thus simply detach from it.

After returning from lunch, I was still surprised at how quickly my perspective about that Instagram post had shifted, at how straightforward this new knowledge was, and at how easy it was for me to detach from my opinion. Thus, I wanted to bring it into use again. This time, I wanted to try it with a more personal opinion, one that it wouldn't be that easy to detach from.

I wondered and wondered, until a point of view that caused me the most prolonged suffering of my whole life emerged. As soon as this opinion flooded my head, hatred seized my heart and spread throughout my body.

At this point, I feared that detachment from it would be impossible to achieve. This opinion has been part of me for so long that it was running through my veins. It also involved what I loved most: my family and my country. It involved thousands of lost lives, millions of families that were destroyed, and more than six million people who have lost their homes, businesses, and jobs while migrating to other countries looking for shelter. This opinion involved the destruction of my beloved country, Venezuela.

Compared to other immigration stories, I had it easier, but it still hurts. I never wanted to leave my country, but somehow, I found myself packing all my belongings into two suitcases more than fifteen years ago. Getting on a plane with the terrible feeling that I would never return, but not even wanting to articulate that feeling, fearing that transforming it into words would somehow turn the worst of my fears into reality.

That plane flew me to France with the excuse of attending a school for my master's degree. When the school was over, I stayed until I married Troy's father, who was American, and we ended up moving to Miami. All the love that grew and continues to grow in me for the countries that welcomed me has never been able to compensate for my loss.

I painfully left everything behind—family, friends, streets, smells, and flavors. I was stripped from everything that was once mine, so it was impossible for me to think that I could stop feeling hatred, repulsion, and judgment towards people (even family members) who supported a government that, during its years in power, had destroyed my entire country.

My reflections on this subject aroused many feelings, and it was a process that took hours and hours of internal debate, so after a while, I needed a break. There was no easy answer; it was clear that this was a problem of attachment, not only to my opinions but also to my country. However, I would first try to detach from my opinions, because I found myself unable to detach from the land that my heart longs for every day. Since I left, there has not been a time when the mention of Venezuela has not brought tears to my eyes.

I didn't want to keep thinking about it. I needed a break. I took a shower and joined the group for a meditation. Then, I went out to the meticulously manicured gardens that preceded the beautiful spectacle of pink and orange skies where the sun was slowly hiding behind the Pacific Ocean. Sunsets have this magical effect on me. Somehow, they make me feel that everything is possible, and with that sweet thought flooding my being, I returned to the room, sat at the small classic wooden desk, and went back to my ordeal.

I decided to ask myself some questions to clarify what was going on inside me. Did I think the people who support the government and the government itself are attached to their point of view? Yes, they were. Was I attached to mine? Yes, I was. Could they change my mind? No, they couldn't. Could I make them change their mind? No, I could not. I was unable to feel their pain, just as they couldn't feel mine.

At the same time, I connected with the hate that has lived inside me for so long, and I asked myself if living the past fifteen years with that hatred has been worth it. My response was, no, it hasn't. As soon as that honest, "no" came out of my lips, I realized that all the hate and pain caused by my attachment to that opinion was useless. It hadn't changed the situation, and it never would. On the contrary, it had tortured me all these years. At this point, I was sure that detachment from my opinion was necessary.

The most challenging part of this detachment process was understanding that I would still have an opinion. I would continue to believe that those presidents and their followers had destroyed my country—I was not that enlightened yet to think otherwise. However, I was going to be able to recognize that this was my simple opinion, an opinion that was not part of me, and by doing so, it no longer had the power to make me suffer. More importantly, I was finally able to understand that my opinion did not prove me right nor prove others wrong.

When night came, I wasn't sure that I was fully detached from that opinion until I was ready to go to bed, and a thought quickly passed through my mind. For the first time in fifteen years, I could see that Venezuela was not only my country but also the one of those who "destroyed it." Therefore, what might seem destroyed to me could be precisely how others wanted it to be. Only then could I see that I should be totally detached from my opinion for a thought like that to cross my mind.

No More Overthinking

Journal entry March 28, 2018: I had one day left of my stay at the retreat, so this morning I explored the idea of the book to which I had committed to write weeks ago. I have been so immersed in all this magic and so enchanted by this new realm, that I had completely ignored that I had embarked on this journey to prove to myself, and now to others, if the statement that changed my life months ago—*Kriya Yoga is a scientific method to achieve enlightenment*—held any truth.

It has been more than seven months since my first meditation and more than five months since my Kriya Yoga initiation. It seemed to me that the time had come for me to answer some questions: After all this time, did I personally believe that Kriya Yoga is a scientific method of enlightenment? And if so, did I have any proof? Could all the sublime experiences that I have perceived along this path account for me being more enlightened?

Although I fervently believe that Kriya Yoga is a scientific method of enlightenment, I still have no evidence to support such a claim, as I haven't reached it yet. I feel I've changed a lot in the last seven months, but I don't know exactly what shifted within me nor how it all happened. I also feel that all the sublime experiences that I have been able to perceive through this path, like my floating sensations, absolute bliss, and pure love would never qualify as evidence of illumination, since I have no power over them, for they simply come and go from my life as they please.

When I started this path, I firmly believed that throughout this year and this process I was going to be magically guided to what to do next with my life...to my highest purpose. And since the end of the semi-sabbatical year is only five months away, I need to make a decision. I need to be totally sure if I will continue with the idea of writing the book. I need to be sure that writing the book is my next project.

The only way I would feel confident about writing about Kriya Yoga as a method of enlightenment is if I find evidence that supports such a statement. Thus, I will use the rest of the day here in the hermitage of Yogananda to look for any proof and in case I cannot find it, I will have to discard the idea of the book and move on.

I continued with my retreat routine of meditating and reading, and during all this time, the need to find evidence ran wildly through my mind. After lunch, I returned to the room, sat at the small desk, and began actively looking for any sign of my transformation.

I began to wonder what had changed within me and to be honest, I had already asked myself that question several times, but I could never find the answer. I knew that something had changed since my closest friends and family had mentioned several times that I was calmer and more relaxed ... and voila, that was the answer.

After thinking about it and analyzing it for a good time. I could feel that yes, I was really much calmer and more relaxed, but it wasn't until I could relive all the despair, tension, and stress of the days prior to Kriya Yoga that it dawned on me the colossal change that had taken place.

I was so excited about this new discovery that I began to quickly explore that past life, and I could remember how in those days I felt stressed and worried about everything. What I found really bizarre was that all that stress and worry came from me. I didn't really have any serious problems in my life. However, my excessive thinking always found a way to turn my little everyday problems into catastrophes that ended up tormenting me greatly.

In those days, I could think about the same problem for hours and hours. For example, if one of my tenants did not pay the rent, I took it very personally. I would harass the poor guy, making three-day notices and posting them immediately. I would talk to my lawyer about the best course of action and get all the documents ready, analyzing second by second any scenario that might occur, and I would be checking the bank account every minute in order to verify if the tenant had paid so the nightmare could end. The drama was not because the money was needed, but because I had no power over my crazy mind.

That erratic behavior not only happened at work but in all aspects of my life, including with my family and friends. I even remember acting this insane in all of my relationships. Any comment that my partner made was psychotically analyzed for the rest of the day. Why did he say that? What did he really mean? I could easily consider twenty different answers to these questions, and in my mind, I would repeat those same scenarios over and over again, and when we saw each other again, I would question him, again and again to find out what he really wanted to say. Because I had spent the whole day thinking about it, it had already become a subject of "extreme importance."

Why did I never realize I was so crazy? Not only did I believe my behavior was normal, but I actually praised myself from time to time for being "analytical" when in reality I was just plain "insane." Why hadn't I noticed that my mind was unleashed, running wild, creating all that chaos and all that negativity within and around me?

In order to establish the basis for others to objectively see and measure the changes that occurred in me thanks to the practice of Kriya Yoga, I needed to assign a percentage to the level of stress I experienced those days and frankly I could not assign any other value that was not between 90 and 99 percent.

At the same time, I needed to assign a percentage to the level of stress I was currently experiencing. I didn't want to be unfair and assign a percentage based on how I felt now when I was in a spiritual retreat. I had to think about how I felt before coming to this retreat when I was surrounded by the mundane, and I could certainly say that I would have estimated that my stress level in those days was between 5 and 10 percent.

After a thoughtful analysis, I could see how the reduction of my stress levels had been caused mainly because my mind was under control and I no longer thought constantly. If my mind wanted to start one of those episodes of endless thinking and excessive analysis, I simply got bored and found it totally unproductive. I wasn't entertained by it anymore.

I wasn't forcing myself to not overthink. It happened so subtly that I hadn't noticed it until now. It was as if unconsciously I had this certainty that no matter how many times I thought about something or how many different episodes I created in my head, everything was going to be all right and therefore all the drama was completely unnecessary.

After realizing what I had unconsciously and effortlessly accomplished in such a short period of time, it seems impossible for me to believe that any of the mundane methods that currently exist could have brought me so subtly to this level of consciousness, because when I tried to control my mind with such methods in the past, my mind has always been ready to dissuade me.

By now, I was very curious about other people's stress levels. I thought that if I wrote in my book that my stress levels were up to 99 percent, nobody would believe me. Since I couldn't talk to anyone, I decided to send a text message to some relatives and closest friends asking them to rate their own stress levels.

When I received their answers, I could see some outrageous numbers as well. I really had no idea that they were under such stress, since they all seemed successful and happy, as if they really knew what they were doing with their lives. The numbers fluctuated between 75 and 98 percent. Right then, I realized that everybody was going through the same problem. Their minds had completely taken over.

Today was a very productive day, not only because I discovered that I could show my advances with numbers, but also because I realized that a book like the one I wanted to write could help thousands of people who were fighting my same battle, people who were not seeking higher consciousness but who wanted to recover that peace that once reigned in their being, by showing meditation as one of the most effective means to calm our minds.

After these dazzling accomplishments, I was taken away by a beautiful state of absolute bliss and enjoyed what was left of the day walking along the beach, until now, when in the middle of the night, I find myself sitting at the same wooden desk writing about this remarkable day.

WHEN I FINALLY LEFT THE ashram the next day, I refused to speak. I felt it was so unnecessary. I walked down the streets and through the airport with a smile on my face, avoiding any kind of conversation, in a catatonic state of absolute bliss. I felt deliciously overwhelmed by all the sudden knowledge that had emerged from me, by all the attachments I had destroyed, and by all the new perspectives of life that I could now see. That trip to Encinitas was the confirmation that a book had to be written. I felt as if Yogananda had given me his blessing.

11

A DEEPER TRANSFORMATION BEGINS

My Detachment from Material Possessions

COMING BACK TO MIAMI, I knew that stressful and mundane weeks were coming ahead. We were supposed to depart at the beginning of June for our three-month vacation to Nicaragua. All the tickets and arrangements were made. I just needed to get through the next two months.

What caused some uneasiness within me was the fact that I needed to sell my house if I didn't want to pay for a mortgage on an empty place during our vacation. We also needed to move out of the apartment we were renting in South Beach in less than a month. We had planned to move to my house until it was sold and then store our belongings until we came back from Nicaragua.

Before starting on this path, I was not quite sure of what a yogi's life entailed. I had always thought that I needed to stop longing for possessions, money, and a nice lifestyle because a "true yogi" or an enlightened person didn't need such things. Over time, I understood that having money and material possessions is not wrong, bad, or evil. It is only our attachment to them that causes all the negativity and pain.

Today it is evident how the Universe has been delicately guiding me to detach myself from money, food, and opinions. However, I cannot deny that during each one of these detachments, everything felt extremely dreadful and painful. I was so viscerally involved with everything I was attached to that I could not see the big picture.

My first failure to detach from material possessions occurred a few months before starting on this path when Joe and I decided to move in together after getting engaged. Troy was going to a school in South Beach, and my house was located in Miami Shores. I was spending more than three hours a day commuting to Troy's school. Joe's job was also located in South Beach, so the most logical decision was to rent an apartment in that area. Although it was evident that it would be practically impossible for me ever to go back to live in Miami Shores, I was so madly attached to the house that, instead of selling it, I decided to rent it out even though the rent wouldn't cover all the expenses of keeping it.

My attachment was so insane that I even made myself believe that the real estate market was going to go up, and thus I would recover all the money I was going to throw away every month trying to hold on to the house. Looking for the cause of this attachment, I remembered that I was raised to believe that owning a house would give me a sense of security and stability, but more importantly, that owning a house meant owning a home.

Although I had been buying, remodeling, and selling apartments since I was twenty-five, I never thought of any of them as my home until I bought that house. It was the first one I called home and the only one I felt was really mine. I had bought it before separating from my ex-husband, as I knew what was coming ahead. That house represented my independence, my freedom, and my shelter —something that I longed for many years.

Those four walls had appeared in my life to protect me during the most difficult years of my life; of course, I was completely attached to them. I had painted each of its walls and planted the hedge around it with my own hands. I had renovated and decorated it to my taste. My brother, Troy, and I had built the cutest treehouse in the backyard. And I also had this beautiful and enormous Royal Poinciana tree with the dreamiest orange foliage that could be seen from every window of the house. How could that tree, that yard, that treehouse, and that whole house not be mine?

I managed to hold on to the house only one more year, because ten months after renting it I received a call from the tenant informing me that she would move out at the end of the lease. I couldn't continue lying to myself, especially after having spent more than six months on this path. This time around, I could see the situation more clearly, and I knew that the smartest decision was to sell. The idea caused me great turmoil for many days. I remember even crying when I finally made the decision; on that day, I understood why all the yoga books talked about attachment. If I hadn't been so tied to that house in the first place, I wouldn't have had this turmoil boiling inside, and I would have made an objective decision from the beginning.

It made no sense to keep the house and keep losing money every month. This time, the plan was to sell it and invest the funds from the proceeds in other income properties, which I needed to do the previous year.

Upon returning from the retreat in Encinitas, I was on a mission to sell the house. I had a month to find a buyer and another to complete all the procedures related to the sale. The house had been on the market for two months already, but I must confess that in my attachment to it, I had unreasonably priced it. So, as soon as I got back, I finally got rid of all its sentimental value and reduced the price.

Once the numbers were adjusted, the house started showing more frequently. Every time I showed it, it hurt because I knew that it was going to sell fast. I declined all the offers that were below the asking price. I remember that on one occasion, I got the feeling that it was going to be the last time I would show it, so I desperately looked for many excuses to avoid it. Yet, the persuasive buyer insisted; he had seen the house before and was now trying to show it to his whole family. So, despite all of my excuses, I found myself on an awful rainy Sunday, heading to show the house to the persistent man's family.

Those strangers entered my house as if it was theirs—selecting bedrooms, deciding on changes, climbing up to the treehouse, sitting on my sofa. I wanted them out, but they seemed to want to stay longer and longer. It was unbearable. I felt that I could lose control at any second, and I could either kick them out or sit down and cry. Therefore, trying to avoid any of those humiliating situations, I excused myself with their Realtor, announcing that I would close the place when I returned.

When I came back, the house was empty. Even though I hadn't received the offer yet, I knew it was no longer mine, that it already belonged to that family. I sat on the sofa looking at everything for the last time and started crying. It seemed so ridiculous to cry over a house, but I couldn't contain myself. I cried and cried until there was nothing else inflicting pain inside, until whatever caused this turmoil had left. The next day the man agreed to pay the full price, and the house was sold.

That episode allowed me to understand how the attachment to material things felt; interestingly, I could recognize that my detachment did not imply that I rejected the idea of buying a house in the future to live in, not at all. It only made me aware not to give sentimental attributes to material stuff, so I can see them for what they are when making decisions.

As I move forward on this path, I see that everything I was hoping to get from material possessions depends only on me, especially my security and independence.

The most challenging part of any detachment process is to notice it, simply because it is impossible to free yourself if you are unable to see the bonds that hold you prisoner. Still, once these become visible, detachment comes naturally, and it is unavoidable.

Only when I am fully enlightened will I attain such detachment that I won't need anything mundane; only on that day will I realize with my whole being that everything I long for is nowhere else but within me. However, today is not that day. I am still far from being fully enlightened. Today is more than enough if I just notice some of my attachments to this world and, with patience, begin to untie myself free.

Developing My Zoom Out Power

One of the skills I have acquired thanks to this path that fascinates me the most is a power which I have assigned the name of "Zoom Out Power."

Before Kriya Yoga, I lived my life in a "zoomed in" mode, like if I had blinders on, and I could only see what was in front of me. In those days, I couldn't disconnect even for one second from what was happening in my life to see the big picture. Life for me was like a walk through a jungle where many surprises awaited and where I never had any idea of what was happening, much less where I was going.

This new skill granted me the ability to consciously separate myself from any situation I was experiencing and zoom out as if

I had become someone else, who was seeing my life from above. Once at a distance, I was able to objectively observe what really happened to me and how everything affected me.

When I use this fascinating skill and I am right above everything, I can see myself immersed in my mundane and meaningless concerns. I also notice how everything that happens to me is temporary and will soon disappear. Then, when I come back down, all the problems that seemed so serious before no longer are.

Welcoming the Self and Surrendering My Control Self-Study

I consider this self-study as the most transcendental on my journey, not only for demonstrating that Kriya Yoga is an effective method to achieve spiritual enlightenment but for opening the doors to my inner world, giving me the most precious present of all: the knowing of myself.

Like most of my self-studies, this one appeared early on in my path, causing a confusion that kept me in the dark for more than six months. It all started when I felt I was becoming careless, not wanting to do my daily activities when scheduled, only when I felt like it. At first, I thought it was simply procrastination, so I didn't write about it in my journal, but, as the matter continued to intensify, I had to rule out procrastination, because it did not look anything like this force that left me totally helpless.

The inner work that took place during this self-study was reflected in a total of eighty-seven journal entries. I had included only the few that show all the anguish and despair I felt when I didn't know what was going on within me. I also have included those that show the distorted explanations constructed by my mind in its attempt to assign meaning to something invisible to my eyes: my spiritual realm.

Journal entry October 8, 2017: I am meditating but not at the same time I used to. I noticed that I want to meditate only when I feel like it, not when I have it on my agenda. I do not follow any schedule set for each activity, and this intensifies every day.

In those days, it was so difficult for me to think that I was gaining something and so easy to believe that I was losing everything, that instead of giving a positive meaning to what was happening to me, I let myself be absorbed by the mundane tendency to see everything negatively. So, instead of understanding that I was finally getting rid of the sick mania of controlling everything, I mundanely believed that I was losing my willpower.

Journal entry November 10, 2017: I'm starting to feel as if my willpower is getting weak. I feel I'm careless. I still want to do all my activities, but only when I feel like it and not when I have scheduled them for. I feel as if I am floating most of the time, and not paying attention to details at work. Before, my willpower was strong enough to keep me meditating, but yesterday I wanted to meditate and got discouraged when I couldn't concentrate, so I stopped after ten minutes when I usually meditate for an hour.

Journal entry December 1, 2017: I have been trying hard to return to my schedule, to meditate, go to yoga, and work at predetermined times. I have even set up alarms on my phone. But I got depressed when I noticed that nothing I had done to fix this issue had worked out. I don't want to end up homeless sleeping on the streets. I have seen people who become so careless that they turn their lives into a complete disaster. I don't want to be like that. I am freaking out. Everything that I have accomplished in life has been due to my strong willpower, so I cannot afford to lose it now.

Journal entry December 19, 2017: Seeing my willpower so weak got me so down that in the last two days, my house was a mess. I didn't feel like I wanted to do anything; nothing inspired me. I have not been writing much in my journal. I don't know how this happened or what I have to do to fix it.

Journal entry January 7, 2018: I discovered that none of the mundane things matter that much to me anymore. What matters to me lately is reading, yoga, meditating, and writing in my journal. My problem is that I want to do them when I feel like it. The fact that they are on my agenda destroys my inspiration. Sometimes I don't feel like meditating early in the morning, so I do it later in the day or late at night.

Journal entry January 19, 2018: This situation has made me lose all my bliss. I am sitting here totally clueless. I have been stressed out by this issue for way too long. This time I will try to do something different to fix it; I will let myself go and do everything as I feel like it—I will meditate, work, and do yoga whenever I want to—and see how that goes. If it still affects me, I will have to stop following this method of enlightenment, because I can't continue like this.

Every day, I woke up with a new plan. Some days, I forced myself to maintain my structure, other days, I was so tired of going against the flow that I let myself go; but as soon as I felt the control and structure were going away altogether, I clung to them to not let them go. Letting go felt like jumping into a turbulent river, knowing that once I leaped, I would have no control over my life, and I was not ready for that.

Journal entry February 1, 2018: Last week, I stopped paying attention to the issue with my willpower. I was waking up at the same time because I had to take Troy to school, and then I would go home, drink some tea, meditate, go to yoga, read, and work. I did everything when I felt like it, without following any specific schedule. I was so happy and so full of bliss, reading, writing, and doing what I love, that things got better. My meditations became super intense, and I felt absolute joy and the love within again.

At that time, I had no idea that my Higher Self and my mind were the ones being affected by this process because, as you can clearly see, my journal entries didn't mention any of this. Instead, they talked about a supposed loss of willpower, of doing things when "I wanted" or when "I felt like it." I never imagined that the part of me which had suddenly appeared, defying my mind, schedules, and customs, was my Higher Self, starting the cumbersome process of emancipation.

I must admit that before beginning this path, I did not understand the interaction between self and mind. In some way, I had mistakenly believed that my mind would always have the reins of my life, thus being the Almighty, and my Higher Self would only manifest when it disagreed. Therefore, I was always proud of my mind for doing an excellent job since my being had only manifested itself on a couple of occasions.

I now understand how all the new ideas, thoughts, and concerns narrated in these journal entries caused the destruction of millions of mundane mental impressions (Samskaras), which had been created throughout my life, supporting the supremacy of the mind over the self. I can also see the formation of new Samskaras filled with Divine Knowledge, that later contributed to give me a more profound understanding of existence, of the self, and its supremacy over the mind.

The importance of this self-study lies not only in losing the habit of controlling everything but in renouncing what caused that sick need: my atheism.

Although at the beginning of this path, I thought that I believed in a Higher Power. I had only experienced that belief on a mental level, because I was still pursuing a completely atheistic existence where the almighty was my mind, the only one with tangible control over my life.

The belief in a Higher Power calls for a conviction in the intangible, which entails taking away all the power assigned to the mind in order to give the reins of our lives to our Higher Self, and that's what was happening backstage during this self-study.

Journal entry March 15, 2018: Today, I took Troy to school very late, and I blew it out of proportion. I blamed myself for not waking up in time, for living this hippie life that will surely lead me to sleep on the streets. How could I continue with the crazy idea of not following any schedule? This incident has sent me back to the spiral of depression in which I had already fallen weeks ago, causing me great pain and irritation. I feel like a loser.

My willpower is weakening again, and the worst part is that I am allowing it. Today I had only taken Troy late to school, but tomorrow something worse could happen, and I wouldn't be able to control it, because by then, I would probably have lost what is left of my willpower.

After more than five months of torture, I felt so desperate that I came to consider stopping my meditations, so I gave myself a few weeks to make a final decision. During those days, I began to ask my masters for guidance whenever I sat down to meditate. That was all I could do at that time. The answer didn't appear immediately, but one day it finally arrived.

Journal entry April 16, 2018: I have been feeling careless again with everything—the cleaning, the way I am eating, the property management, and the accounting. This morning I sat down after the meditation and began to analyze the issue. This time the analysis was different. I reminded myself that I had asked for open eyes and for this path to lead me into a new life. So, if I had asked for such a significant change, I should expect a substantial transformation—something considerable to shake my life up so I could finally open my eyes to a new reality.

If I think about it, I can see that what creates this anxiety is not following a schedule or not having everything done within the time I consider best, because at the end of the day, everything is being done. My meditation is done every day, sometimes in the afternoon or at night, but sooner or later it gets done, and the same happens with my other activities.

If I look back to previous times, I can see that my life revolved around always following plans and timelines; I never had time to "live," instead I just accomplished tasks. Before, when a tenant moved out of one of my units, I generated a lot of stress on myself trying to have the unit ready as fast as possible, scheduling all the necessary vendors for getting the unit ready. I pushed the vendors to work as fast as they could in order to have the unit ready and back on the market immediately, and then I tortured myself trying to have the unit rented in no time. Surprisingly, while I created all that unbearable tension in my life I didn't even notice it because my stress levels were already too high. Stress was already a big part of my life, a big part of who I was.

However, after just these few months of walking on this path of enlightenment, if I do something a bit stressful, I can feel it in my body: in my stomach, throat, and chest. I am fully aware that it is something that is not part of me. Today, I can see the difference because when I get to do the same job, I don't feel like following all those crazy deadlines or calling vendors right away. I prefer to do it when I have the time. I also notice that I am not in a rush. I treat the vendors right, without pushing them with unrealistic demands or deadlines. So, why do I consider this new approach to be careless? What would it take, two or three more days to finish the property? How much would those two or three more days cost me? Isn't it better to lose that money, rather than generating all the negativity in my body and with the people that work with me?

That day, I managed to discard all the reasoning that once seemed logical to me, and I finally jumped into the turbulent waters. It was right then or never. I decided to do everything whenever I felt like it, to let everything flow, and not to force things. I did not give myself the opportunity of a plan B, because I was already confident that this was the way to go.

Ironically, after several weeks of letting go, I felt guided by a strange force that managed to fit every piece of my life magically into place, without any effort or stress on my part.

When I let myself get carried away by that strange energy, my mind showed doubts. The most challenging part wasn't trusting in the process but believing that going against everything that I have learned and experienced in the past was the right thing to do.

The outstanding change that had taken place within me was invisible in the midst of the darkness in which I lived. My level of consciousness in those days was not high enough to perceive any transformation.

Only when I started writing this book and saw through my journal entries the person I used to be, I could finally grasp the radical change that had occurred within me. More than a year had passed since that transformation. During that year, meditation had raised my consciousness, allowing me to see a completely different reality from what I described in my journals. I could finally comprehend that what had produced the insane need to control everything was my mind, and so I deduced that if my brain no longer had the reins of my life, it meant that my Higher Self had regained its throne.

I also learned that unlike my mind, my Higher Self didn't control anything. Thus, instead of keeping me within the confines of my body, my Higher Self had broken down all the barriers that separated me from the world around me. There was no longer interior or exterior. The essence of everything in the Universe was exactly the same essence that conformed my being.

Everything I got with the emancipation of my Higher Self drastically changed the way I experienced the world around me. It also allowed me to completely abandon the archaic belief that I was careless if I did not follow a schedule. Instead, I was able to understand that most of the time, when I refused to follow a program, I was unknowingly in contact with internal and external forces that I had never felt before.

While working on this section of the book, I recognized that being guided by my Higher Self is the way to live a more open and conscious existence. It makes us one with the flow of life and takes us to the most unexpected places, opening us to experiences that we would never have otherwise. Being guided by this energy has been the most incredible adventure I have ever been on, an adventure that you will be able to behold as you advance through the book.

Gone is my mundane idea that in order to know myself I had to know what I wanted or where to go in life. This path has connected me with the only thing that matters, with my essence, with the Supreme Power that exists within me, with what scientists call "God's particle."

The subtle glow that now lit my path showed me that the secret to enlightenment doesn't lie only in the means used to obtain it, but in our ability to recognize and enjoy that beautiful journey giving us endless sparkles, always shifting and always dazzling. I finally realized that Yogananda had never referred to enlightenment in the sense of a destination but as the most fascinating journey of our lives.

12

COSTA RICA

IT ALL STARTED after returning from Hawaii. That magical little green dot in the vast Pacific Ocean had left us with a memory that refused to be forgotten. Everything there felt so natural, so alive, so destined to be, that we couldn't wait to experience more of it—more of that magic that you only perceive when you let your guard down and surrender yourself to what only the Universe can offer.

After returning from the dazzling spell we experienced in Hawaii, we couldn't help but feel trapped by our routines. We had already experienced what it meant to live our lives to the fullest, and the way we were living in Miami was not it. There was no comfort or mundane beauty that could compete with having the time to experience the connection with our beings, with nature, and with everything around us.

With these thoughts running wildly in our heads, we started to dream about our next destination. This time, we knew that two weeks or even a month would not be enough. We wanted to extend it to make it last as long as we could, and that's how the dream of a three-month vacation started to form in our minds.

At first, that idea sounded scandalous even to me; regardless, I had the flexibility to work from home and set my schedule. The most extended vacation I had enjoyed lately had been a month and a half, and most of the people around me were already scandalized with the fact that I took forty-five days of vacation. I had only had the pleasure of a trip that lasted three months once, and this happened more than twenty years ago when I first visited Europe with my siblings. Still, somehow, after all these years, a vacation like that sounded off-limits, as if only the wealthiest of people or backpackers without responsibilities could afford it. Not working for three months while splurging on vacation sounded too good to be true.

On that first day, when this seductive idea surfaced, we flirted with it all night long. We talked and talked until our exhaustion brought us back to reality; by then, we couldn't do anything else but drop it as if it was a dress displayed in a window shop that you try on but decide you can't afford, even though you have the money.

The next morning, as always, I couldn't let it go. To me, all of this was starting to sound too good not to be true. Like in all of my dreams, I knew that I only needed to unlock the secret to making it happen. At the same time, there was something about us thinking a vacation like that was impossible that got me intrigued.

We both had money saved, and we could easily afford it, so why did it sound so outrageous? Was it because people around us weren't doing it, that made it seem it wasn't normal? Perhaps we believed that we did not deserve it or preferred the security of having money in the bank instead. Well... I have to confess that it was all of the above.

Those thoughts immediately connected me to that three-month vacation in Europe with my brother and sister, which is, to this day, the most enriching experience of my life. We had absolutely nothing, but we weren't worried about it, we lived every second of those ninety days to the fullest. We experienced the exotic taste of freedom as we watched our wildest dreams come true, defying all odds. Three siblings born and raised surrounded by nothing but favelas in Caracas drove from Madrid to Barcelona, passed through the French Riviera, and crossed Monaco and Italy, to end up in Paris.

In those days, we were only concerned with experiencing life to the fullest, as if we knew that real life and worries would always be there waiting for us when we returned. Time was the only thing we had, and it felt so good to have it. We did not mind sleeping in the car to avoid staying in depressing low-cost hotels in order to save the money needed to extend the trip and visit more places. Life was easy, full, and well-lived... When had it all changed?

Where did this need come from, to comply with what others were doing only because it seemed normal and reasonable? Why did we need to fear tomorrow just because everyone else did? What is the point of having money if we don't enjoy it because it is safer to live a mediocre life, instead of living an inspired one today without obsessing about tomorrow? What a sad way to live. We might still have a few years left before going to our deathbed, why not make them all count?

At this point, I already knew, without a doubt, that the trip was going to happen. Maybe if I made it look cheaper, we could trick ourselves into believing that it was okay and wouldn't sound so bad to our old conservative minds. I was just starting my enlightenment path and semi-sabbatical year, but a trip seemed like the best way to end it.

By the end of the day, I had already come up with a plan. Rather than paying two rents (one in Miami and at the vacation destination), we would cancel our lease in Miami in early summer and store all of our belongings. This way, we could save enough money to support ourselves for almost three months in any other less expensive place, spending the same that we would have spent if we stayed in Miami.

After some research on lodging, flights, and costs of living, I presented the plan to Joe as soon as he returned from work. It was at that very moment that he realized that it was going to happen. The idea immediately lit up his face, leading him to suddenly confess that he hadn't stopped thinking about it all day at work. There was no convincing involved. It was as if both of our beings had secretly made a pact the night before, and we had been shown the ropes to make it happen.

The spark in his eyes and the smile on his face is all I can remember from that night. After that, our starless Miami nights revolved around planning for that long-awaited summer. Joe's terrible days at work didn't seem so burdensome anymore, for they had acquired a new meaning.

Once the real plans began, we chose a small, inexpensive surf town in Nicaragua, and right before the end of 2017, all the reservations were made. All we needed to do was wait for the first week of June.

The day of our departure was fast approaching. I had miraculously sold my house just in time, and most of our stuff was locked in a small storage unit in Midtown. For the first time in the last ten years, I had no home or place to return to, and for the first time in my life, I appreciated it. I felt so weightless. All of our essential belongings fitted in the four suitcases scattered around the floor of the Airbnb in South Beach we had rented for our last week in Miami before summer arrived.

I remember finding myself in that living room, submerged in delicious stillness but still amazed by the wrath of the hectic month that had just passed, yet still weightless. That lightness was such an exquisite and delicate sensation that I wanted it to continue infinitely saturating my whole being... I wanted to enjoy it until its last drop... I had nothing physically tying me down anymore. I had no possessions, and my investment portfolio consisted of some numbers on a spreadsheet. I had no attachment to it; even the car I was driving was a lease. I could have never guessed that renouncing most of my possessions would feel this good. I emptied a part of me that had been cluttered for many years, and I was now able to breathe deeply and float much higher.

After a full day of enjoying this sensation and finishing the last details for our departure, we watched as the news of political unrest in Nicaragua began to intensify. We contacted people who lived there and confirmed it was unsafe to travel with a seven-year-old. There were shortages of gas, protests, and blocked streets. Two days before our departure, we decided to change the destination, and during those two days, we needed to find a new location, cancel and get refunds from all our reservations, and make new ones.

Fortunately, everything worked out fine, and all of the refunds were made. However, the flights could only be changed to Costa Rica or other Central American countries. We chose Costa Rica because it was the one with the most consistent surf waves, and that's how what started as three months in Nicaragua ended up as three months in Costa Rica.

The Country

Costa Rica is more mystical and magical than any other place I have ever been to. From the first contact, it presents itself with such a modest grandeur that it leaves you puzzled, totally unable to find a word to describe it. Absorbed by this ambivalence, you find yourself going deeper and deeper into rawness, where no signs, no pavement, and no warnings can reach, where only a deep yearning can take you. Walking through what seem unexplored areas, your senses come alive, awakened by this rawness as if they had always belonged to this place. And, if you dare to walk a little bit farther and let yourself go, you will come to understand the meaning of the pureness in it all—what they call Pura Vida—realizing then that this is a place that you would never want to leave.

Forcing Myself to Be on a Higher Level of Consciousness

Costa Rica has become a place very, very dear to my heart. However, I must confess that it was not love at first sight. It all started those last two days in Miami when we were looking for a new place to stay. Joe had chosen a small surf town in the Guanacaste Province, where we decided to stay for the first two weeks, and once there, we would look for our next destination.

By then, I had been on this path for more than ten months already. Unfortunately, I believed that I was more advanced than what I really was on a spiritual plane. My recent detachment from material possessions somehow led me to believe that I was already fully separated from the mundane and on a much higher level of consciousness when, in reality, I was pretty far from this. I still had a long way to go. I guess I needed to experience it to believe it.

As I felt light as a feather by my newfound detachment from material possessions, it occurred to me that comfort, appearance, and space were things that I could live without as well. Therefore, while making reservations for our first two weeks in Costa Rica, it did not seem unreasonable to think that we could stay with a seven-year-old in the middle of the Costa Rican rainforest in a hotel with rooms made out of shipping containers.

The hotel looked nicely done. It was at "walking distance" from the beach and the town. I read several comments and did my own search on Google Maps. The previous guests were very happy, and the place seemed to be a few meters from the beach, according to the map, which meant freedom to walk everywhere without the need to rent a car. And as you must be anticipating now, it was all a disaster.

As soon as we arrived at the airport in Liberia, Joe tried in vain to convince me again to rent a car. Drowned by my detachment delusion, I rejected his suggestion one last time, and we proceeded to fill the first taxi we could find with our four suitcases and four surfboards. It took almost two hours to get to the small town. After the first hour, the paved road was never to be seen again. The closer we got, the more scattered the houses seemed, with fewer people and cars.

When we finally arrived at the minuscule town, we noticed that there were no taxis. The closest to it were tuk-tuks that served the few tourists who came to that remote place. This realization made me feel very irresponsible for bringing Troy along without a vehicle. What if something happened and we needed to go to the doctor? I started to breathe deeply to help the stress go away. By this time, our taxi driver started to drive up a mountain. At every turn, I anticipated a descent, but no, there was no descent—the hotel was on top of the hill. The only thing passing through my mind upon arrival was the image of us walking up and down the hill with our longboards every day, and from what I could see, going down that hill was not going to take ten minutes, as the website stated.

Once in the hotel, I was furious. I felt totally deceived. The hotel was minimal, and when I say minimal, I mean everything seemed like half the size of what was shown in the pictures. Even the paths to go to the reception area and the little pool needed to be walked sideways, not to mention we didn't even have a full container for a room. No, our shipping container was separated in two by a wall, which meant we were staying in half of a container. In my mind, everything was a rip-off, and you might think that at least we should have saved money... but no, the price of that half-container was the same price that you would pay for a four-star hotel in South Beach two blocks away from the beach.

Of course, when we got to our room/half-container, Troy's first concern was the little spiders walking on the walls, which immediately translated into having Troy sleeping with me and kicking me all night. As soon as I pictured this scene, I couldn't take it anymore. I had been holding it in for too long. Everything... everything was wrong. Luckily, I didn't explode, but I told Joe as calmly as possible that I wasn't going to stay there, that we needed to find somewhere else to stay.

How could I fall so low from higher consciousness to this? I felt like one of those nasty people that leave the ugliest of reviews on Airbnb. The poor Argentinian guy that was left there to manage/cook/host was so sweet and so helpful that it broke my heart to show him my disappointment with the place. I needed fresh air.

We put most of our belongings in the half-container, because of course all of our stuff couldn't fit inside, and decided to get that much-needed fresh air while discovering the town. When we were ready to leave the place, the manager let us know (since he saw us with Troy) that it would be better to take a tuk-tuk. At this time, I was trying my best to breathe through my nose. I knew that if I opened my mouth, something very nasty was going to escape.

We called the tuk-tuk, which arrived right away and took us to the center of town. Surprisingly, we found a fantastic vegan restaurant on the beach. I was forcing myself to look only at the positive side of things, hoping that would help me face the not-so-good parts of the journey.

After lunch, we walked to the beach, which was not my kind of beach as the water was brown and the sand black. At this point, I continued even harder to suppress my hostile attitude. We walked up to the side of the beach where our hotel was supposed to be. Joe and Troy played soccer with some locals, and we decided to start going up to find the hotel before it got dark.

As soon as we started the ascent, everything went pitch-black. The sun had disappeared entirely, there were no lights on the road, and we could only hear what seemed like ferocious dogs barking at us from every house. After walking and walking with no idea where we were going, we started to freak out. At some point, we even lost track of the route back to the beach. Luckily, Joe had asked the tuk-tuk boy to give us his phone number. Joe called him, and he came to our rescue in no time. We arrived back at the container, took a shower, and went to sleep...and that was our first night in my beloved Costa Rica.

The next day, I had mixed feelings, so we decided to hold off on moving to another hotel. The breakfast was terrific, and the server/manager/cook was still super sweet. After breakfast, we started our thirty-five-minute walk to the beach, each carrying a longboard. The beach didn't help much either, as it was not suited for beginners. We spent three days like that, and each one of those days, I complained about every little thing that I found was "not right." After those three days, we had explored every little place in town. I tried my hardest to battle against complaining about the whole situation, but I was in a terrible mood most of the time and was definitely not enjoying the vacation fully.

At that moment, I had two options: to lie to myself, believing that I could stay there while having the worst vacation of my life or accepting the reality in which I was still bound to this mundane world. I couldn't deny that I needed comfort, space, a car, hot water, a beach with blue waters and white sand. I needed to accept all of it and stop forcing myself to pretend that I wasn't affected by it.

I decided to be true to myself. I talked to Joe, and we decided to stay only ten days instead of fifteen, using the remaining time to finish discovering that part of Costa Rica. We rented a golf cart for the rest of the days, and we had a blast—well, Troy had a blast, as he was driving for the first time. We visited Bodhi Tree, a fantastic yoga and retreat place close by, and discovered beautiful and unique beaches with amazing sunsets. By the end of the week, I had already forgotten my reaction from the first few days. We started to fall in love with the place, and with the hotel I hated in the beginning.

My morning meditations at their little yoga shala, which was suspended in the middle of the jungle among the tallest and greenest trees I have ever seen, were plain magical. There, I was able to feel the aliveness of nature, how it breathes, how every living thing out there was in perfect harmony with it all. At the beach, my meditations were so grounding. For the first time, I felt while meditating on the beach, an incredible force coming from the ground, connecting with me through my root chakra, allowing me to feel like part of this earth.

When the time to leave arrived, we were all full of mixed emotions. The rawness of the place had touched us in the depths of our beings, forming threads that would always be there, but we were also aware that we would not remain sane for much longer if we stayed.

What we lived on those days was similar to what I had experienced walking on this road when I sometimes pretended to be at a higher level of consciousness. I had often forced myself to do things just because they were the most conscious things to do— like not worrying about how I dressed up or stop using nail polish or makeup for good—when instead I only needed to advance a little more each day on this path, organically and subtly.

I must learn to choose my battles, but at the same time take fewer but more grounding steps. Frankly, I wasn't ready to disconnect from everything, and much less being with Troy. The plans were made, and our next adventure was taking us to another surf town with better waves one hour away.

Detachment from My Country

Driving along the semi-paved road in this bigger town made us feel as if we were back to civilization. We looked out the car window as if we had been locked in the jungle for months. There were shops, people walking down the streets, plenty of restaurants, surf shops, and some pavement. We checked into our Airbnb house, which seemed like a palace to us after our previous experience.

There, our real vacation started. We could unwind; we were no longer in survival mode. Our days consisted of waking up, having breakfast at home, and spending most of the day at the beach. We would eat lunch at one of the restaurants by the beach and then return home to shower and rest. In the afternoon, we would walk through the town for coffee or ice cream and then go back home to have dinner, drink some wine, and stare at the starlit sky.

Being in that paradise, without much to do, would make you think that my complaints would stop. Instead, this time around, all of my criticism was redirected to the country, Costa Rica. I found myself asking questions like, "Why are the prices thirty percent higher than Miami if half of the town does not even have paved roads?" I also generalized the fact that some locals tried to take advantage of us for being tourists. Other times, I simply complained about the waves not being good enough, or about the beaches being too crowded. Every day I had something bad to say about the place and the country.

I must confess that I was oblivious to this continuous complaining until Joe pointed it out once I came back from Miami after I dropped Troy off so he could spend the rest of the summer with his father.

Although hearing Joe's remarks helped me notice my constant dissatisfaction, I couldn't figure out the why behind it, so I dropped the issue, completely unaware that my "why" would be revealed to me in a few days.

A week later, we were surfing Playa Negra, a beach surrounded by a voluptuous jungle, which had become our favorite surf spot, regardless of the two-hour drive through unpaved roads full of potholes to get there.

That day driving back home, we were so stoked from a great day of surfing that we couldn't wipe the smiles off our faces. The windows were down, the music was blasting, and Joe was amusing himself trying to avoid the craters on the road while going as fast as he could in the poor rental car.

I remember that my sister's Spotify playlist was on, and while Joe was having fun with the car, I took the opportunity to sing along —out of tune as usual. During those minutes, life was simple, sweet, and full. However, when the next song started playing, my mood changed instantaneously. The new song was titled "Mi Felicidad" by Nacho and Víctor Muñoz, a beautifully composed song about the hopes of returning to the country where you were born and grew up, a country that, no matter how far away, still runs through your veins and makes your heart beat.

As soon as the song started playing, I felt my heart deflating until it felt like a prune. The pain was so intense that in a couple of seconds, it invaded my whole chest and inundated my eyes with tears. I guessed the sudden outburst was partly caused by the surroundings, as this road reminded me of a path leading to a surfer's beach called Choroni in Venezuela.

As the song played, I couldn't stop looking around, and through my eyes filled with tears, I was still able to see the incredible vegetation that surrounded us. Everything there seemed so alive, so wild, so free. But I didn't want to be in a place that looked like my country... I wanted to be in my country. The more these thoughts went through my mind, the faster the tears came. I didn't want Joe to see me cry. I didn't want to explain what was happening to me. I just wanted to experience it, so I suffocated my pain and smothered my sobs while tears still welled up in my eyes and flew wildly in all directions carried by the wind.

Perhaps... that was the reason for all that negativity towards Costa Rica; maybe its similarity to my country accentuated my loss. There was so much pain locked in my heart, a pain that I had never wanted to let out. Because the times when I was not able to contain it, it had burst into my life, feeling like a fresh open wound, so fresh that you wouldn't be able to notice that more than fifteen years had passed since its heartbreaking infliction.

If you had asked me at the time if I wanted that wound to heal, I would have frankly said no. I wanted that pain to stay with me. It was like a morbid way of always being able to reconnect with the pain of having to leave my country. It was as if by having all this pain still latent locked within prevented me from forgetting Venezuela. To be honest, it was also a kind of self-punishment for having abandoned her in the hands of others. Tears continued to flow abundantly and desperately as if escaping from a bottomless pit. The wind blew my hair while a lump in my throat, accompanied by a helpless feeling, barely allowed me to breathe.

I recalled how I had previously worked on the attachment to my opinion towards what happened in my country and the people who I believed caused all the destruction. But this pain was completely different; it was not caused by others' opinions and who did what...this wasn't important to me anymore. This pain did not include hatred, just a sense of loss, as if I had been stripped of my country and as if it would never be mine again. And that was the reality, because the country I loved, the one in which I grew up, would never return, I had completely lost it. And yet, I still love Venezuela, I love her as one of those passionate Latin love affairs, like the ones that you lose your head over and fill your veins with. I love her with this crazy infatuation that blinds my eyes and blurs my mind.

The song had already finished, and something else was playing. After a while, there were no more tears. The well had dried up. I felt as if the nature that surrounded us had heard my choked cries and felt my tears, and in return, gave me the warmest of hugs. I finally understood that I had to let her go. Two lonely tears escaped when I realized that she had never been mine, the only thing I could do from now on was to love her and to love her with detachment.

I can't deny I still cry every time I remember her, every time I talk about her, but the sense of loss that consumed me is gone. The wound has slowly healed and become a scar. The pain and the powerlessness have disappeared. Yet, I still find myself waiting for the day when I can walk through those streets, bathe in those waters, and live again on that land, even if this happens in the last days of my existence.

Several days after such profound emotions, I started to notice that I no longer complained about Costa Rica. All that vast space previously occupied by pain and a sense of loss was now filled by this new love for Costa Rica, the land that helped me heal.

13

NEW DISCOVERIES, NEW EXPERIENCES:
THE PRESENT OF SURFING

I HAD ALWAYS THOUGHT the path to Higher Consciousness was a path of renunciation, and not only to the material and mundane, but also to the excitement, fun, sex, and living a passionate life. However, after more than a year and a half following it, I had discovered it was exactly the opposite of renunciation. Instead, I found it is a path of openness to new worlds and new experiences because it is only under the light of this newness that all limitations disappear, allowing us to feel our being in the purest of its forms.

Kriya Yoga has allowed me to experience more profound layers of joy, happiness, and passion, layers so intense and so deep within me that I would have never been able to connect with them any other way. Today I find excitement, profound joy, and inspiration every time I am suddenly carried by seconds of bliss and pure love, or when this path secretly guides me to connect with new places, people, or experiences.

I still remember how, before that trip to the Big Sur, I was tired of feeling the same emotions over and over again. In those days, I concluded that there weren't any new feelings left within me, that I had already felt everything that was to be felt, and life had become kind of stagnant to me. Looking around, I noticed that everyone lived similarly, so, over time, I resigned myself to believe that life was based only on those repetitive and limited emotions. At that time. I couldn't understand that if our days consist of doing the same thing again and again, we would always experience the same emotions again and again.

Surfing has been one of those beautiful realms that I discovered while walking on this path to higher consciousness. All of a sudden, it has become this newness that makes my heart beat faster, that novelty that I think about day and night, one that allows me not only to experience nature but also to be one with it.

For those hours, the entire world disappears, and the only thing left behind is my body floating on this magic artifact that grants me one of the most precious presents of all... to become water. I become the sea. I become the waves, moved by the unseen forces of the tide, shaped by the wind and by what lies beneath. When I am there, I become a drop in the vast ocean, and this connection is as beautiful and intense as the sweetest of my meditation states. At sea, I can recognize my essence in every-thing that surrounds me, and it is a recognition that brings so much light and sparks back into my life that I spend all of my days counting down the minutes until I become water again.

Again, my love for surfing wasn't love at first sight. This romance began immediately after leaving Troy in Miami to spend the rest of the summer with his father. Upon returning to Costa Rica, Joe and I created a small routine where our days revolved around high tide. The three hours prior to high tide were strictly devoted to surfing, and everything else was scattered around in the remaining time. In my case, the rest of the time fluctuated between writing my book and meditating while Joe indulged in massages, yoga, and reading *Autobiography of a Yogi*.

One day, after two weeks of following this routine, when I had already been surfing for two months, we were coming back from a sunset surfing session, and for some reason, I couldn't contain it anymore and exploded. I was frustrated with surfing and had kept it a secret with the hopes that the feeling would dissipate. But that day, all the accumulated frustration found its way out. I told Joe that I was quitting surfing, that it didn't make sense to me, that it wasn't my thing.

In those two months, we had been in Costa Rica; I had religiously gone to the beach every day to surf, giving it my best. Yet each one of those days was a battle, a battle that, of course, I had lost. Whenever a surf session ended, I would come out of the water either with a bruise or with blood gushing out from some part of my body. Sometimes I just dragged my ego out of the water as my exhausted and sore body couldn't continue to endure those tiring sessions of trial and error. In every one of those sixty days, I felt like a complete loser, as if I was so clumsy, so non-athletic that I couldn't get right something that seemed so simple and graceful. The only thing that kept me going for that long was my meditation, my strong will, and of course, Joe.

The most frustrating and challenging part was reading and catching the wave. To be specific, my only advancement was being able to stand up on the board and go straight, but I could only catch one out of thirty waves when trying my hardest. I had built up an extraordinary strength paddling, as that was what most of my days of surfing consisted of. Every day I surfed, I spent most of my time paddling my hardest to get on a wave, missing it, then going back to the lineup—and that was if I was lucky and wasn't dragged back to shore where the breaking waves made it almost impossible to return.

That day, when I exploded, I honestly couldn't take it any longer. It was one of those days when the sea is so furious that it doesn't want anyone in its waters, and if you are fool enough to defy its will, you will be spit out offshore as many times as you can bear it. However, I was so focused on practicing that I was completely unable to zoom out, see the whole picture, and notice that it just wasn't a good day for a beginner surfer. The only thing I could see once I got out of the water was how my stubbornness had dragged me along for two months, making me lose my time on something that I would never understand when I could have spent all that time surrounded by nature, enjoying writing my book, and meditating—things that I was comfortable with.

After all the time I dedicated to learning how to surf, I still wasn't as hypnotized with surfing as Joe was. He could spend every single day at the beach surfing his hours away, and when he was not in the water, he was talking about being in the water or on his phone watching surf videos. I remember that even when we met, I was immediately aware of his passionate love for surfing. However, only with time, I began to desire some of that craziness, some of that impulse that inspired him to surf. Maybe that was the reason that I tried it for that long.

I still remember when the phrase "I don't want to surf anymore" came out of my lips, decorated with a tone of defeat. Joe looked at me for a few seconds and replied, "Okay, okay." That was an answer I wasn't expecting, so I was a little confused. *Why wasn't he trying to convince me to keep surfing?* Maybe he had noticed how difficult it was for me, or how far I was from actually getting it... perhaps he knew there was no point for me to continue trying. All of those thoughts were immediately interrupted by him talking about a surf shop in town; this was the fourth time in the last couple of days that he had mentioned this store. He had been there while I was in Miami, dropping Troy off, and was obviously impressed with it.

He was talking with such passion about the place and its Argentinian owner, who hand-shaped each of his surfboards, that it seemed as if me quitting surfing wasn't a big deal. The reality was that I was relieved—relieved that he didn't care and relieved that he didn't try to push me into continuing. When I came back from my thoughts, he was still talking about the surf shop. This time the monologue had moved on and was now centered on the idea of buying another surfboard. At that time, he had four boards, and there he was, thinking about buying another one. I remember thinking that he had lost his mind. The last thing we needed was another board, especially now that I was quitting surfing.

He tried to explain it to me, but in my mind, the concept of shape, volume, or two inches more or less to improve the surf didn't make any sense. All I could think of was that we needed to get rid of all the boards that we were not using, especially mine. It was as if Joe could read my mind because soon after, he suggested that he would sell all four of the boards to buy this new board he was so infatuated with. Flying back to Miami with one board instead of four sounded ideal, so when he asked me to come along the next day to visit the surf shop, I happily accepted.

We were at the surf shop early in the morning. The store was a massive contrast to the dirt roads that surrounded it. The name couldn't be anything other than Cheboards, considering that Che is a typical Argentinian substitute for dude. From the moment I stepped into the store, I could feel the owner's love for what he does. Everything was so well laid out, so well thought out, that the store seemed more of an art gallery than a surf shop. I was impressed. Only then was I able to understand Joe's infatuation with the place. Each one of the surfboards was, in fact, an art piece, so delicate, so perfect, that they seemed to be made with nothing but love, heart, and dedication. It was as if a little piece of the artist was in each one of them. When I turned around to look back at Joe, he was as excited as a boy in a candy store.

Joe talked to the salesperson for what seemed an eternity. I had no idea what he was talking about, but it seemed like a lot of explanation for a simple surfboard. Eventually, Juan Diego, the owner/artist, came out from the shaping room in the back to talk with Joe. Juan Diego was even more passionate about surfing than Joe; they spoke to each other as if they were long-time friends who hadn't seen each other since they were kids. They talked all about surfing, the places to go, the waves, and the surfboards. They were so stoked that they didn't even realize that the saleswoman had left and that I was sitting on a bench, looking at them with a puzzled face. It seemed that for them, everything around had entirely disappeared.

The interaction between these two adults, who spoke with the enthusiasm of two children, intrigued me greatly. I had always thought Joe's obsession with surfing wasn't normal, but now this man had appeared out of the blue talking about surfing with even more passion than him. While these two adults were talking at what seemed like 100 words per minute, I tried to figure out why. *Are they both crazy or is this surfing thing really good? How come when I tried it, there was so much suffering in it for me? Did I do something wrong? Could it be that I was not persistent enough in its practice?* I remember even wondering if the board was the problem.

When Joe and Juan Diego noticed that I was lost in my thoughts and tried to get me involved in their conversation, I had nothing nice to say about surfing, so I kept quiet. Joe then asked Juan Diego to enlighten me about the boards. They had been talking about the Lightning Bolt brand and how they had chosen Juan Diego for his craftsmanship to shape some of their boards. The speedy conversation soon shifted to Witch's Rock, a surf spot a few miles from Tamarindo, where the '80s movie *Endless Summer II* was filmed. I guess Juan Diego noticed I was clueless to every word he was saying because he happily grabbed a book and started to explain through the pictures in it the golden era of surfing and those old-school days when longboards were "the boards."

As he was talking to me, I could see his eyes beaming. His words were coming out of his mouth so fast and in such a passionate way that I could barely make sense of any of it, and to be sincere, the only thing that was passing through my mind at that time was how something as simple as surfing could have these two grown men so inspired. Not even winning the lottery can make someone vibe this way for this long. The energy that they were producing together was so intoxicating that it continued to keep me completely confused. After what seemed like an eternity to me, Joe asked Juan Diego if he could try one of his boards. Juan Diego replied that he had a used Lightning Bolt board at his house that he could let him try. We drove with Juan Diego to his house and borrowed the board. Joe had injured his back recently and planned to stay out of the water for a couple of days until he felt better.

We went back to our place, still vibing with Juan Diego's energy. It isn't that often that you can meet truthful and down-to-earth artists. These days, if someone has any kind of talent, it all goes pretty fast to their head. Thus, meeting an authentic artist so inspired by his craft and so accessible has become something rare to find.

I couldn't stop looking at the board in our living room, with these two questions playing on repeat in my mind: *How could we meet such an inspiring dude the day after I quit surfing? And would a good surfboard make that big of a difference?* I was so intrigued that when Joe asked me if I wanted to try the board, I was already in my bathing suit.

We went to a beach close by. The tide wasn't perfect, and the waves were rather small; the only thing I had in my favor was the absence of wind, resulting in a glassy water. As soon as I got on the board and started paddling, I noticed that I was sliding through the water with almost no effort on my part. It was only when I caught the first wave that I could experience the caliber of the board beneath me. I got the wave almost automatically, effortlessly even. I popped up and stood up with no problem. For the first time in my life, I could steer the board in the direction I wanted, trimming the wave... what a feeling!!! All those months of skateboarding had finally paid off. With the previous board, I wasn't even able to turn. I couldn't believe it; everything was as smooth as if I was surfing on butter.

I was so excited that I started to scream at Joe, "This board is amazing!" And right then, surfing those mini waves on that glassy water with the luminous Creamsicle rays of the sun setting behind me, I fell madly in love with surfing. I knew I was hooked. I didn't want to get out of the water. I wanted to stay there forever, and although there were not many waves, I felt like, with that board, I could surf them all.

During those hours, I felt like a child again; I went back to those early childhood days when you discover something new and become so addicted to it that your mom has to force you to stop. That day, I understood that I could spend the rest of my days surfing my life away. As night fell, I couldn't stop talking about the magic of that day. The inspiring energy of Juan Diego had blasted into our lives, vibrating with the highest of levels, and with the present of his art, I could see this other world, and in it, everything seemed so bright, so simple, and so right. No other activity in my life had ever produced such an intoxicating feeling as surfing did. Because even when every inch of my body was completely exhausted, I had remained in the water wanting more and more.

This present reminded me that I have so much more to experience, that a Universe full of new experiences and feelings awaits. The more I was out there waiting, floating, and feeling, the more I noticed the wind, the colors, the water, the sun. Little by little,

I understood that surfing isn't a battle, as I always believed. Not at all. Surfing is simply an expression of our connection with it all. The more you are out there, open and feeling this connection, the more you begin to understand everything—the effects of the wind, the tide, and the moon. With time, you begin to predict what will happen, how the wave is going to react, and how it will treat you. At some point, you also start to notice those days when the sea doesn't want to be ridden, as it becomes intolerant and harsh, and if you are strongly connected to it, you do nothing but respect it and give it its time.

Surfing has given me so much. It has given me a connection with nature and with my body, as well as the realization that every single wave I am able to ride is nothing more than a present from the Universe, granting me the honor to become one with it. Most of the time, when I am in the lineup, I don't want to sit up like most surfers. I just lie down on the board with my ear pressed against the fiberglass to quietly listen to the nothingness of the underwater realm while with the other ear, I capture the sounds of the world I live in. And it is right there, on that borderline, that I also feel part of both worlds. So I just lie there, patiently floating, waiting for the next set.

When in the past, I was ruffled and moved from side to side, looking for the perfect spot to get waves, I now feel the waves follow me. I feel as if they somehow know me and are attracted to me.

Few people know that waves move energy and not water, as they are the medium through which kinetic energy circulates. Therefore, I can only attribute to that fact the thrill I experience every time that thanks to the board, I become that force carried by the waves. That electrifying and inexplicable sensation begins once I have given everything I have and surrendered, since I know it depends only on that water to decide if it allows me to travel with it, to be it. And magically, it all happens, and I am propelled. Although astounded, I stand up, riding it, trying to be weightless and unnoticed, because in those minutes every inch and every movement counts.

Some days, if I am lucky, I don't have to wait for a wave. I become one with the sea from the moment my feet touch the water, and I begin to submerge myself in the warm and salty liquid. I also become one with the air that caresses me, with the seagulls that glide around me, and with the mountains that look at me from a distance. Thus I am given the power to be the entire Universe. This exhilarating connection with it all is what has all of us hooked, stoked, and ready to experience it again and again and again... Surfing is, without a doubt, one of the most natural of the drugs we could ever get addicted to.

How This Path Guided Me to My Highest Purpose

Do what inspires you instead of what you love...

The drafting of this book began while I was in Costa Rica when everything revolved around the high tide. Today, ten months later, when I am a few pages away from its completion, I find myself astounded, wordless by the realization that the book is practically done, even though I have been dreaming about this moment for a long time already. It has been a long journey, and I'm certain that without all of the time and the pondering locked in the conception of these pages, I would have never realized the power of the journey I embarked on twenty months ago.

To be honest with you, the first day I started writing this book, I panicked. I was there for hours and hours with the computer on my lap trying to type something, anything I could think of, on these white pages, but nothing... nothing came up. I was blocked. The reality was that I wasn't a writer, I had never written anything, and I have never studied or taken writing classes. Yet there I was with my hands over the keyboard, trying with all my heart to embark on this adventure.

During those excruciating hours in front of my computer with nothing but a white page on the screen, I couldn't help but think about the infeasibility of the task I had asked myself to accomplish months ago. At some point, during these hours, a crazy cycle started, where I timidly typed something that soon after was rapidly erased. After several repetitions of that nonsense, and after the night appeared, laughing at the fact that my all-day effort had ended up with the same empty page, I started to feel like something was taking over me. Suddenly, out of nowhere after all of those hours, inspiration arrived. And it barged in like a raging storm, inundating every space of my mind. Unable to be contained, it downpoured on the pages that minutes before were white and lifeless.

I found myself glued to the chair, typing every thought that was rapidly overflowing my mind as fast as I could. The hours passed, the moon was gone, the sun was rising, and I was still typing away totally inebriated by a sweet elixir that I have never tasted before: inspiration.

Since that night, I found myself under its influence, counting the minutes until its arrival and rushing my fingers over the keyboard, afraid of its departure. There were days I couldn't stop until Joe appeared as a link to a world I had escaped from. Other days I woke up in the middle of the night engulfed by it and quietly ran to another room to type away until my eyelids unconsciously closed.

In those days, which I considered the most fulfilling days of my existence, I wrote the entire backbone of this book. However, when I got to what was supposed to be the last section at that time, "The Present of Surfing," I could not ignore that something was missing. Although the book clearly demonstrated the changes that occurred to me thanks to the practice of Kriya

Yoga and revealed the secret to knowing ourselves, it was missing something that I somehow believed would be unveiled along this path: what to do next with my life, my highest purpose.

I only had one more week in Costa Rica, after which, not only my vacation was going to be over, but my semi-sabbatical year would also come to an end. I should have already received an indication of my Highest Purpose by now, and I certainly did. I had received all the signs, and they were all there, right in front of me, but for some reason, I wasn't able to see them.

In the early days of this journey, when *Autobiography of a Yogi* had found its way to me, I was at a point in my life where I had no idea what to do next. I had already closed my brokerage and felt suspended in the air, waiting for any hint that guided me to the next chapter. I remember feeling the idea of "do what you love" touted by motivational speakers and self-help books was the one that got me into my brokerage business mess in the first place.

Before opening that business, I had spent more than a year trying to figure out what I would love to do next, which resulted in having dozens of new ideas per day and, at the same time, feeling scared by overthinking what could go wrong in all of them. All of those ideas and fears were pulling me in different directions.

After all that time, I decided that making money with real estate was the closest thing to a profession that I loved, as I had always loved the rush and excitement I got from making deals happen. So I convinced myself to continue in that direction. It took more than two years for me to have everything ready, and during all that time, I wasn't able to wake up from that illusion and avoid the imminent crash. The reality was that being afraid of inaction and terrified to dive deeper within me to discover who I was, led me in the wrong direction for more than four years, resulting in a waste of time, effort, and money.

How was it impossible for me to realize that I urgently needed to know myself deeper instead of finding another way to make a living? Even when I started on this path, I had not realized that I needed to know myself. At that time, I only trusted that this enlightenment process would guide me into what to do next, and to figure out my highest purpose. I was sure that if you have at least an iota of enlightenment, you must know what to do with your life. I firmly trusted this belief. I didn't know how, but I was sure it would happen. I was so confident that I had even forgotten about it until today when the missing part of my book and my life has come to be exactly that: What to do next?

When I started to think about it again, I sensed something was different this time around. I had a weird feeling as if I already knew what to do with my life, as if it was on the tip of my tongue. I was so confused and exhausted by all of these strange ideas that I had to take a break. I remember I looked around, trying my hardest to ease my being. The huge branches above me reminded me of the paradise I had been in for almost three months. How unreal it was for me to be there, in Costa Rica, a place that I would have never chosen to visit, but where I had experienced such an intense awakening and where I had lived the life I had always wanted to live. It was just after that last thought crossed my mind that I was able to see it all. I was living the life I had wished to live that New Year's Eve in Amsterdam. That wish had become a reality. I was living a harmonious and peaceful life filled with inspiration, and I was absolutely fulfilled by it.

I quickly noticed that writing represented a considerable part of that harmonious, peaceful, and fulfilled life. Right there with tears of happiness, it became evident to me that I couldn't live the rest of my life without writing. At that moment, I finally understood everything: writing was my Highest Purpose, what I was guided to do since the early days of this path. I was amazed by the discovery, but then I started to remember that Sunday when I was guided to the ashram in Homestead, and how feeling guided led me to write this book. I also remembered how difficult it was to start writing, and how inspiration had come at the last minute, to save me and show me that it would always be there when I needed it.

While lost in those beautiful memories, my skeptical mind started screaming: *Have you completely lost your mind? You are not a writer... hello? Do you know that people study for years to be a writer? In case you haven't noticed, it's actually a profession! Do you really think that you are good at it? This terrible idea that has got into you is just a waste of time, and sooner or later, you will end up eating up all your savings pursuing this crazy dream.* As my mind ranted at me, I felt as if this episode was a déjà vu, transporting me back to a day in my childhood, when I was a girl of about Troy's age. I managed to connect with that part of my life that I was not aware of, a part that had been buried someplace within me for all these years.

The scene I was recalling was similar to the one I had experienced seconds before when my mind was trying to make me understand that writing was not for me. However, this time the sermon included that being an author was a profession that did not guarantee a stable income. The episode took me by surprise; I wasn't aware that moment even existed until this exact second, so I began to search in my past for more clues, wondering why did I want to be a writer at such a young age? Why had a dream that seemed so intense been buried within me for so many years? Slowly, I was able to salvage some of that fascinating past that seemed so intriguing today, and I began to relive those days that ended up becoming the best days of my childhood.

I remembered that I was part of that generation that did not have access to video games or the Internet; the only means of entertainment at home were television and books. I also remembered that by fifth grade, I had started to love school again. My mom worked full time, which meant that we had to stay at home by ourselves after school. Since I was the oldest, I was considered the one in charge when my parents were not around. We lived on the thirteenth floor of an apartment building, totally surrounded by favelas; however, amid that chaos, enclosed within the walls of that small apartment, was the most valuable treasure a kid could have when growing up. One of the four walls of the living room was a beautifully crafted built-in bookshelf that contained a collection of over 200 books.

The wood finishes of this private library seemed so delicate that it immediately contrasted with the zinc roofs and exposed brick shanties that could be seen from the window. I never understood how that intriguing wall space had gotten there, but I always assumed that it was my father who had had it installed so he could display his book collection.

Half of the books were encyclopedias, which at that time were our form of Google, with the difference being that you needed to work a lot harder to find the answers. My brother was fascinated with the *Encyclopedia Britannica World Atlas* that contained all the maps and all the information of every country. By the age of nine, he knew every country and capital in the world, most of the wars fought, and the reasons that started each one of them. I was obsessed with an encyclopedia that consisted of twenty volumes, a Hispanic adaptation of *The Children's Encyclopedia* by Arthur Mee, entitled *El Tesoro de la Juventud*. The compilation included different sections, such as "History of the Earth," "Countries and their Customs," "Book of Poetry," "French Lessons," "History of Famous Books," and many others.

I still remember climbing up to the highest shelves to get more books. We could spend hours and hours lost in them. By the time I was ten, I had already read most of the books that were interesting to me, mostly related to art, and I started to be lured by more advanced books. I remember that there was one that interested me enormously because I was captivated right from its first pages. It was a special edition, with a brown hardcover with its title *Chronicle of a Death Foretold* by Gabriel García Márquez in golden letters.

Despite my age, I wasn't a novice reader. I had read most of the encyclopedias in that library and managed to read them without a dictionary on hand. However, when I started to get immersed in that book, I recall asking my mother the meaning of at least one word per line, until I finally understood that not even she knew the meaning of some of the terms used by this genius author. The richness of the language and the magical way he described reality was something new to me, something that made me feel gently and slowly transported within each of his stories, and once there, I was delighted, touched by each one of his words. I had never again read anything like it—until later when I was introduced to Amélie Nothomb's books in France.

My encounter with Gabriel García Márquez's novels at such a young age made me fall in love with the limitlessness of the lettered realm while being initiated into voluptuous and passionate Hispanic literature.

I fell in love with school again, especially with language arts. My teacher then noticed it and fostered my love for reading and my newfound passion for writing. I started to write with such inspiration that one day after a special mention from my teacher on one of my papers, I realized that writing was what I wanted to do for the rest of my life. I wanted a life that revolved around books, not only to read them but also to be an author. For me, that seemed to be the answer to living the best life.

Unfortunately, I could also remember how that inspiration and that dream were little by little suffocated until they were ultimately forgotten. The more I grew up and got immersed in the mundane world, the more those favelas that I could see from the windows started to lose their charisma and became a stigma of who I was. I soon saw them in correlation with my value. Dreams of literature, art, and culture were quickly replaced by the only way I could come up with to get out of the slums, which was a steady job and hard work. Thus, when a decision needed to be made, I chose to study accounting, and my childhood dream was buried immediately, until those days in Costa Rica when I was able to live an exquisite version of that fantasy. Whimsically, that chimera seemed to emerge from my being's deepest places, opening all the windows, letting me feel all the light, all the air. And it all felt so right, so meant to be.

I have no doubt this is my Highest Purpose. There is no other way for me to live life except by being surrounded by this magic, by this inspiration, by my first dream. This time, the mundane world has lost its grip on me. What moves me to write today is not money. No, what drives me today is inspiration, this ethereal force that moves my fingers across the keyboard so rapidly, as if there wasn't enough life to live my purpose. That day in Costa Rica, there was no decision to make. I just needed to get back what the mundane world had once taken from me.

When I look back on everything that happened to me through this path, I recall situations and presents given to me by the Universe like Jack Johnson and Pablo Alborán's performances or visiting Juan Diego's surf shop. In each of those gifts, I can recognize the Universe trying to show me that it was possible to live a life full of inspiration, where everything moves slower, and everything is intensely felt. In that new realm, the word "work," which reminds us of our ties to the mundane, vanishes, allowing us to reach the highest expression of ourselves...creation.

14

THE DARK NIGHT OF THE SOUL

ALTHOUGH MY IDEA was to recount only the first year of my journey to higher consciousness, after seeing how my second year unfolded, it became imperative to include it as part of this book. While the first year was full of light, magic, and synchronicities, the second was in contrast filled with such darkness that made it almost impossible to see any magic, signs, or connections. I knew I was at a higher level of consciousness than in the previous year, but it felt as if somehow I had to start from scratch at this new level.

I had never heard of the term "the dark night of the soul" before. The first time was while I was visiting the ashram in Homestead, two and a half years after being initiated. On that Sunday afternoon, after our group meditation, I heard several people talking about the term during lunchtime. From what I could understand, it seemed a widespread concept among people looking for higher consciousness. Although I could not intervene in the conversation because I had previously committed to a week of silence, I listened attentively.

According to everyone present, the uncanny name was given to one of the initial stages of the enlightenment journey and was preceded by another phase called "absolute bliss." The duration of each one of these stages varied enormously in the eyes of everyone present. Yet, they all agreed that during the dark night, all the happiness and all the magic perceived in the previous phase disappears altogether.

That conversation, heard by chance, allowed me to give a name to the phases I had experienced so far through my journey. I could see that my "absolute bliss" phase started when I read *Autobiography of a Yogi* and lasted until we finished our vacations in Costa Rica. My dark night unlike most of the stories I heard that afternoon in the ashram, didn't last three, four, or six months; mine spread over an entire year, and it started right after I came back to Miami from our vacation in Costa Rica until the end of the following summer.

Listening to others narrating something similar to what I had already experienced filled me with rare tranquility. Walking on this path without anyone there to guide you fosters in you the sensation of being alone. It also leads you into thinking that everything you are experiencing is not real, that it is just a plain invention of your mind. Still, when others confirm they have had access to similar situations or experiences, it's difficult to avoid feeling that you are not alone, that everything lived is real, and that you are undoubtedly on the right track.

While I was sitting on the floor, listening to those who were around me, I couldn't help but remember, when in that same ashram and on that same patio, a young girl confided to me all the magic she was experiencing, validating with her story all the magic in mine. How improbable was the fact that about a year later, this new conversation was corroborating a phase where the opposite happened, where all the magic vanished? Even though it seems inconceivable, my euphoria was the same. That mysterious conversation confirmed that although the magic had not been there to guide me, I was still on an enlightened path.

Magic Disappears

When we returned to Miami after our vacation in Costa Rica, it was extremely difficult for me to adapt to the mundane again. After all the magic lived during that summer, I suddenly found myself back in the city, longing for the greens and blues that had sheltered me for so many days and the simplicity of my life in those faraway dirt road towns.

My semi-sabbatical year had come to an end, and during that year, the Universe had led me to live the life I had secretly always wanted to live. Writing my days away was a pleasure that I could never call work even if it filled up all of my hours. I had planned to continue managing the properties without getting involved in any additional work until the book was completed. I wasn't worried about what to do at the end of that period since I had learned to let myself be surprised by the Universe. In the meantime, I just enjoyed the pleasure of writing. This book became my everything, my today, my now, a precious part of my life.

I had been meditating daily for more than a year by then, and this was a practice to which I continued to devote fervently one hour of every one of my days. My relationship with meditation had changed dramatically from that first year, when at times, I forced myself to meditate to cross it off my list, flourishing into this delicious activity to which I now devoted myself vehemently, without any thinking or forcing involved, even without planning it. I only felt my being calling, so I lit up incense and sat quietly to empty my mind.

Although meditating became essential to me, almost like breathing, eating, or sleeping, after returning from Costa Rica, I began to notice that my practice had lost the intensity of the first year. I initially tried not to stress about it, since I believed it was all part of the pendulum effect. After everything I experienced in

Costa Rica, it was evident that it would take me a while to regain that much-needed balance. But, by January 2019, after more than five months, my patience had dissipated entirely, leaving me with the feeling of not being able to bear it. Not only had the intensity of my meditations decreased, but the magic and synchronicities that lit my way the past year were less frequent.

Many times during this period, my mind tortured me with the idea that my life had taken a wrong turn, away from the enlightened life I wanted to live. When this happened, I simply clung to all the beauty this path had previously shown me. I tried my hardest to believe that everything that was happening to me was simply an internal process in which it was impossible to see the light until it ended. At this time, I was clueless to the fact that this process was only starting and that I still had more than six months of tourture ahead of me.

Dealing with Negativity and Detaching from People

This self-study began its chaos in mid-November 2018. However, it was not until the last day of April 2019 that it finally exploded in my face. That day, I remember being overwhelmed by a deep sense of defeat while composing the book segment where I share the birth of my niece and describe feeling that pure love that abides within all of us.

I remember sitting there, writing about the most sublime and elevated experience of my life, but feeling like a con artist in the midst of it all. It felt as if everything I was writing in this book was a lie, as if I wasn't more enlightened. How could I have an iota of enlightenment if I couldn't even deal with some people? What was the point of having sublime experiences if I was still affected by the downs of life? Let me backup a little and provide more context...

A couple of hours before this breakdown, while I was at my desk typing frantically, accompanied by my friend inspiration who had come to visit me earlier, I was bombarded with spiteful text messages from a very dear relative. The reason behind those texts was as crazy as any you might find in a soap opera. It had no beginning, no end, and of course, it made no sense, but for some reason, I was in the epicenter of it all. (I don't know if it's just me, but every time I play a part in a soap opera, I feel like I'm doing something terribly wrong with my life to end up there.)

Since I did not want my inspiration to drift away, I ignored all the drama overflowing from my phone. I was clueless to the fact that as soon as my inspiration started its departure and I had the time to think about what had happened, I wouldn't be able to keep it together, and I would break down.

To be clear, that wasn't the first time this dear family member involved me in one of her soap operas; this was already the eighth time in the past six months. Each of these episodes could last weeks, days, or hours. It was as if the life of this beloved person was so chaotic that it always had to blow up, and most of the time I was, unfortunately, close by when this happened.

The first time I was involved in one of these episodes was five months before, and of course, I did not have the slightest idea what was happening. However, in the eyes of my dear relative, I was the only one to blame for the entire situation. Thinking that it was just a fleeting thing, I ignored the incident, disregarding the fact that I was unjustly mistreated. These episodes began to occur more frequently, and I continued to ignore them. The situation then reached a point where I felt a desperate need to do something about it, as it had already begun to disturb my peace, harmony, and even my meditations.

I had never experienced such intense negativity or such a crazy soap opera since my divorce. But in it, I was the star, the craziest of the entire cast. This soap opera was different because I had nothing to do with it, so why was I involved in it?

After many unsuccessful conversations and draining almost all the resources I could find to terminate this madness, I tried my last resort. I ventured with something I have discovered by walking on this path and that I use when I don't know what to do. This technique consisted of trying to find my answers in nature. So, I asked myself, How does nature react when something like this occurs? I usually look at the sea, the sky, the animals, and the plants. Most of the time, I am able to find the answer I am looking for. In this case, I was specifically concerned about how to react towards those who appear in our lives, trying to direct all their stress and negativity towards us. Should I accept it as I have been doing, until it disappears the same way it appeared? Should I recognize that the situation affects me and fight against it? Or maybe I just have to decide to stay away from that person.

I remember looking around for weeks without finding an answer. The Universe seemed to be working in perfect harmony. I couldn't see anything like it anywhere, until a weekend when Troy was invited to a friend's birthday party at the Lion Country Safari in West Palm Beach. There, in one of the exhibits, was a huge iguana locked in a cage with some small monkeys, one of which was happily jumping on top of the iguana's head. What caught my attention was that the iguana did not seem to care. It didn't move. It didn't even blink an eye, so the monkey just kept jumping.

At this moment, I remembered my question and thought: *It can't be!! I have to take it, like this iguana!* But soon after, the iguana could no longer put up with it and just walked away. The monkey, unaffected, began to jump elsewhere. Only at that moment was I able to see the answer I was looking for. I didn't have to put up with this. I just needed to walk away.

For me, walking away wasn't as easy as the iguana made it seem. I loved this person, she was part of my family, and I had been raised believing that family was the most important thing, you just don't get rid of family. Clearly, walking away was not an option for me, so I ignored the wise message of nature and continued to endure all the new episodes of the soap opera.

After this brief explanation, let's go back to the day I felt like a con artist, the day when I had just finished dealing with the most recent episode of this soap opera and was bombarded with text messages while writing part of this book. At that moment, I felt abused and helpless. In less than two hours, this dear relative had not just turned my life upside down but was threatening to prove the invalidity of the scientific method of enlightenment I had been working for more than one year.

I felt like I was losing everything. This issue was far beyond "not being affected by it" and was more like being destroyed by it. My despair was such that I knew I could not sleep that night. Troy was staying at his dad's for the weekend, so I went to his room to avoid waking Joe up.

There I was, on Troy's bed, wondering if all the magic I had experienced the previous year had been a sham. As much as I tried, I couldn't think about the scientific method of enlightenment, because at that time I was only an addict who needed her drug, and at that time, my drug was all the drama I was involved in.

I had the idea tosend a text in which I let this person know how I felt. This time, I would try another approach explaining how I felt these episodes as aggression towards me. I also wanted to address the significance of our relationship to me, and finally, apologize if something I had done in the past could have caused all this bad energy between us.

As the writing began, a feeling of helplessness washed over me. This emotion was so intense that I could not continue writing. I suddenly felt trapped and paralyzed while tears started to stream down my face. Those tears caught me off guard, and as they poured, I understood that I did not want to do anything that would push this person out of my life. My attachment to her had dragged me into a destructive relationship and kept me indifferent to the fact that I was being abused. I was crippled by this discovery, and by the fact that it was so easy for me to ignore my own mistreatment, little did it matter the intensity of it because no degree of abuse should be acceptable.

After several minutes of not crying, the last two tears welled up in my eyes. Those lonely tears took me by surprise, but as they slowly went down my cheeks. I could understand that they had escaped from inside because I felt hurt, deeply hurt by someone I loved. I was so locked up at that moment, gripping at it so intensely, that more tears started to come out of my eyes. However, this crying was not helpless as before. These were tears of pure pain, and only when I was able to recognize this, I felt an explosion within me, as if my heart was a delicate crystal ball that had suddenly broken into a thousand pieces.

As I was crying inconsolably, I felt as if a huge weight was being lifted from me. I was suddenly relieved from an invisible pain that seemed to have always been in my chest. The knot that tied me to her was slowly being undone as if I was releasing her, and as if she was releasing me. Only then could I clearly see how attached I was to her and how the clues that nature had given me previously contained the whole truth.

I knew that text would never be sent, as all the helplessness and pain were gone. My chest and heart were finally open. I knew I would always love her even though I was totally detached from her, but this love without attachment gave me freedom. It was three in the morning, and I no longer wanted to think about what had happened, so I put down my phone and immediately fell asleep.

The next day, bliss finally came back to my life. The previous day's episode seemed as if it had happened ages ago, like a scar with no pain. But I was mostly relieved because the con artist idea had fled my mind. Surprisingly, I was more confident on this path than ever before as I was able to recognize that what I experienced all those months was simply part of the process, part of the road, and part of this present from the Universe.

Why a present? Well, because for the first time in my life, I was able to take my blinders off and understand that, whenever tears and pain appear, there's nothing else behind it but pure and raw attachment; even though we can't or don't want to see it, it is there. I had always thought that I wasn't attached to people, and yet, there I was.

The Self-Study with No Name

I was aware that the magic had finally appeared to guide the last detachment, letting in the bliss I had been longing for so long. But I also knew that it all would soon go away, and I would return to my simple life, exempt from magical experiences and sublime perceptions, and that was precisely what happened.

After a couple of days, as all the beauty disappeared, I was left with a strange sensation. Something in my life was not right. I could recognize how this sensation had been on a sneaky rise since I came back from Costa Rica, but I never paid much attention to it. All of my previous self-studies had a name, but this one awakened something that was buried so deep within me that I couldn't see it, much less name it.

What I found to be consistent with previous self-studies was the fact that I felt invaded by a strong discouragement. I started paying little attention to household chores, relationships, and work. I only enjoyed the time I spent with Troy after school and the writing of this book. I somehow knew that all the dullness and depression indicated that the lesson approaching was one of enormous proportions.

I didn't know it back then, but this self-study involved the destruction of several layers that concealed my true self, making it the most painful and liberating process I experienced along this path.

The Endless Book

My days continued to drift, sitting in front of my laptop, writing the pages embodying this book. Inspiration had become my ally and visited me frequently. I could spend more than ten hours in front of the screen typing, without noticing the passing of time. Troy's father had begun spending more time with him, which allowed me to disconnect myself from the mundane and fully surrender to these lines from early in the morning until late at night when Joe came home from work. Sometimes I stayed at home for the entire week writing until Troy was returned to me.

In those hours, I was utterly absorbed by the beauty and magic of the kingdoms I tried to recreate in these pages. The inspiration brought into my life by the writing of this book was like a drug I could not quit. These pages had become the only place where I could get in touch with the magic that had become so difficult to perceive, so I locked myself in them for days on end.

At times, I thought this alienation from the mundane was a problem, and that perhaps I was confusing inspiration with obsession, creating an attachment to the book. So, I began to give some space and time to the manuscript for it to develop organically. Even when it has been me who spent entire nights and days writing each word contained in these pages and experiencing all the stories recreated in them, I have always felt as if this book was not mine, as if it had a life of its own. I was under the impression that this book had always wanted to be written and had used me as the means for its materialization.

So every time that I, excited by some sections of the book, felt the anxiety to finish it to share my discoveries and experiences, I remembered that the book was not mine and that ironically it was not me who had the last word about it. So, I took a deep breath and kept giving it time because as bizarre as it might sound, the book itself was the only one that knew its content and when it would reach the moment of its completion.

By the summer of 2019, after writing everything I considered needed to be shared. I had the sensation that the book was still not finished, that something was missing. I was so confused that I even sent the manuscript for editing, believing that if I saw it ready to print, I would experience that long-awaited feeling of completion. However, when the edited manuscript was returned to me, there was still something lacking, and I still had no idea what it was. By this time, Joe and I had planned to spend the next two months of summer in our beloved Costa Rica for the second time. So, I decided to wait until we came back. Maybe the time away would help me to decipher what was going on with the book.

Costa Rica as a Catalyst

Costa Rica intensified everything that was happening within me. In that country, I was able to confirm that even having a very intense connection with my Self and being guided by it, my vibration was entirely out of tune with everything around me, including nature.

In my surfing, I could clearly feel this disconnection. I had bought a new board from Juan Diego, which I was really eager to try, but since the first time I got in the water, my experience was quite different from the one I had with the previous board. The problem, of course, wasn't the board, it was me. I spent several weeks trying to adapt, but I couldn't see what I was doing wrong, until one day I gave up and decided to hire an instructor to start from scratch.

In the following days, I was able to notice that the whole problem revolved around my disconnection, not only with the board, but with the sea, the waves, and the wind. I recognized that I was trying to surf mechanically, putting my hands in the right place, trying to catch the wave at the right time, and in a perfect way. I was actually surfing with my mind, and surfing is the complete opposite of that, and much more like meditation. You have to disconnect from your mind and just feel it. In surfing, there is nothing logically perfect, only moments that feel perfect, and therefore they just are. It only took this realization to recover my surfing gradually; after a couple of weeks, I began to surf like never before, with so much grace and so much love that I felt like dancing on the board.

This experience with my surfing reminded me that, even when I get disconnected, I also have the power to straighten whatever is crooked in my life to connect again. I knew that the Universe had again sent me a sign... to feel more and think less, in order to find my answers. With this in mind, I decided to discover what had caused the absence of magic and bliss the last year. Then, it was easy for me to see how my anguish and stress about this issue had triggered an alarm since the beginning of my dark night that made me try to look for answers with my mind when all I needed to do was to "feel" what was happening.

For several days I tried to feel what this year without magic, connection, and bliss had meant to me. Somehow, I felt that all of it was simply part of the path. Back then, I did not know that those who embarked on a path to higher consciousness commonly experience this type of disconnection, much less that this period was widely known as the dark night of the soul.

As my days and ponderings continued, I began to notice how not being guided by the Universe through magic and signs implied being directed to look for it inward, blindly trusting in my being. It was as if the path was indicating to stop waiting for magic, absolute bliss, and answers to come my way, that it was time for me to figure out how to find them within. Perhaps this was the way the Universe showed me that nobody else but "us" were the creators of everything in it, including that magic I desperately craved.

The end of this second trip to Costa Rica marked the end of my dark night. Curiously, during those last days, my meditations became of extraordinary intensity, saturated with a force that I had never experienced. Every meditation filled me with immeasurable power, which dissipated every time I opened my eyes, and the practice came to an end. This contrast aroused great curiosity within me. I had the impression that something had been developing within me during these two years of continuous meditations, and I was sure that it was related to the ability to perceive that powerful force within me.

Many days passed, and my curiosity began to grow excessively. One day I took my laptop and locked myself in one of the rooms of the house. I was determined to get to the bottom of the enigma. I decided to write down everything I had learned about meditation because I had an inkling that within me existed a knowledge of which I was not aware, but that could clarify the whole matter.

I decided to start with a question that had always intrigued me and that even after two years of daily meditations, I thought I had no answer for: How does meditation work? To be honest, I imagined that simple, absurd, and even illogical ideas would come out of me initially, becoming a bit more sophisticated with time. To my surprise, ideas that I didn't even know I had began to come out quickly and articulately. For more than a week, I locked myself in that room to write day and night, stopping only to eat and surf. In the end, I wrote more than ten pages that today constitute the Afterword to this book and the tangible consequences of my dark night.

I felt as if each of those eight days had calmed my anguish. When it all finished, I no longer expected to find elusive moments of magic, absolute bliss, or any other divine perception. I had realized that within me was something much more valuable, a divine knowledge that provided me with the clarity I had desired my whole life, one that would increase as I progressed along this path.

The knowledge revealed by my dark night was so intense and radical that it illuminated aspects of my life that seemed fine in the dark, but that showed cracks under this new light. It was as if I could no longer lie to myself, as if I had always known those cracks were there but had decided not to look at them, thinking that this simple omission could make them disappear. Although I could no longer deny what was happening, I didn't even want to estimate the damage that could be caused by all the fractures I was able to see now. Especially when one of those cracked aspects of my life involved my relationship with the man I was in love with, the man with whom I had decided to share my life and that of my son.

Although my relationship with Joe was beautiful, it involved many sacrifices on both sides. In my case, all those extreme concessions were simply the externalization of something much more serious happening within. This was the "self-study with no name" that had tormented me for more than six months already.

I spent several days ignoring everything I could now see, and in that state of forced inertia, I spent the last days of my vacations in Costa Rica. The land that saw me leaving the previous summer experiencing a dreamed life, one year later saw me saying my goodbyes with my head down, trying to delay the imminent fall that would mark the beginning of a long journey towards a more elevated understanding of romantic relationships.

15

MY DETACHMENT FROM ROMANTIC RELATIONSHIPS

The Beginning of the End

THE SAME DAY we arrived back in Miami, I made plans with my dear aunt, Nidia, and my friend Julia, who were vacationing together in the Sunshine State. We arranged to meet the day after my arrival. I wanted to do something special for them and, at the same time, have them taste a bit of the magical world I had been immersed in thanks to the practice of meditation—and I knew who to turn to to make it happen. I immediately contacted my friend Perla to organize a private session of her "Breathing Experience" practice at home.

Perla is one of those friends that you ask the Universe for when you start on a new path—when the friends of the person you used to be begin to disappear from your life because you have nothing in common anymore. Our kids were in the same class in second grade, but it wasn't until recently when I went to one of her breathing events that we finally connected and were interested in getting to know each other better. Perla was on a path similar to mine, so we had many things in common, which made our conversations deep, interesting, and always revealing.

My first breathing experience had been seven months ago, and it had been an unforgettable experience. Thanks to that exercise, I remember that I managed to reach a high state of being similar to those I achieve during intense meditations. What I love the most about these exercises is that unlike meditation, you don't need many sessions to connect with the divine energy within. Often, the first time you try it, you can reach states that some meditation practitioners only achieved after many meditations. I usually invite people who have never experienced anything outside of the mundane, hoping this practice would show them fragments of a more ethereal world.

The Answers Appear

It was time for our breathing session. I was very excited about the moment we were all about to share. Being honest, I was not anticipating perceiving anything during the exercise, as I was more interested in having those I invited get the most out of this fantastic experience.

It all started as usual. I had become very familiar with the breathing, the music, and letting it all go. It was the fourth time I attended one of these practices, and even though in some of those sessions I had gained divine insights, I never felt anything different from what I perceived with my meditations, but that was about to change.

A few minutes after starting the exercise, a tingling sensation surfaced throughout my body. This shy feeling quickly trans-formed into a powerful energy, vibrating with more intensity in my hands and feet. I had already felt similar sensations before, so I was still very calm. However, after several minutes, something unexpected happened.

Tears began to frantically come out of my eyes, and uncontrol-lable sobs emerged from my mouth, while my body kept shaking violently with intense pain. I was shocked. I had never expected anything like it. The pain emanating from me in such a hasty way was unlike any other. My heart was being squeezed with no mercy, and even though I wanted to stop all that madness, it was impossible. I had utterly lost grip of my emotions and my body, so everything just continued to come out. The music accompanying the exercise was blasting out from every speaker in the living room; still, my desperate and painful cry could be heard by everyone.

After what seemed like a couple of minutes, I tried again to calm down as I felt deeply ashamed with my family and friends. I was trying in vain to stifle my sobs when I heard my friend Julia crying in the distance. So I decided to stop my useless efforts as I felt somehow accompanied in my pain. My body was still at the mercy of the experience. I waited, believing this embarrassing incident would end soon. I couldn't be more mistaken because immediately, pushing through my inconsolable sobbing, my inner pandemonium emerged. Enormous bonds within me started to tear apart while deep roots were furiously pulled out from the deepest places. Inexplicably, everything within me had turned into chaos and devastation. After several minutes of this madness, as all destruction ceased, my tears continued to flow, washing away all that was left.

Although I had already experienced something similar before, the pain I felt from this detachment was much more intense than any other experienced along this path. The undone knots and the roots were so massive that I didn't know if they had left anything else within me when this was over. I could easily predict by the magnitude of the pain and the destruction caused that this episode was related to my relationship with Joe and to the self-study that began to unveil weeks earlier towards the end of my vacation to Costa Rica.

When my sobs and tears no longer emerged, and my body was suspended in nothingness, I felt myself entering a chamber deep within my mind. In this place, there was a dark room, where I could see various mental clips repeating incessantly. I knew they were all related to the sudden detachment I was experiencing. By taking a closer look at those clips, I recognized that they all marked significant moments in my life. These mental impressions had formed my knowledge and perception of relationships, marriage, life, and happiness.

In the first clip, I could see myself playing with a doll at a very young age, saying, "When your Prince Charming appears, you will get married and live happily ever after." Another clip repeated a scene that occurred just after my divorce, where I was sitting on my bed, thinking that the next time I found a person that I loved, I would have to commit to making more sacrifices to make the relationship work. The last clip contained a scene from our recent trip to Costa Rica when, while sitting alone in bed after an altercation I had with Joe, the idea of separating passed through my mind. However, without even thinking about it, I had dismissed it quickly, as if leaving Joe was something impossible. By connecting with this scene and delving into its meaning, I realized that I was holding onto that relationship with everything I had because, sadly, I had always been afraid of being alone.

That fear must have been hidden in the deepest and darkest place within my mind, silently, pretending not to be part of me, for I had never realized its existence. I never saw myself as a woman who believed in fairy tales, happy endings, or who expected to be rescued by a Prince Charming, and much less as someone who was scared of being alone. I always felt that I was a strong woman who could make difficult decisions and face their consequences. I could see now how those perceptions and fears manipulated my existence from the shadows.

When I came out of that chamber, tears still ran down my cheeks, but they had been transformed, from tears of pain and despair to tears of relief and gratitude. It felt like being under a cascade, whose waters healed everything fractured within me during that detachment. I wanted to continue experiencing that restorative cleanse. I was not ready to leave that state and face everything that would happen by being consistent with the revelations I had obtained.

After an hour had passed, we were guided back to this world. When I finally felt my body was returned to me, tears were still drying on my temples. I had cried throughout the entire session.

As we all subtly tried to recover from our own experiences, several minutes passed with no word uttered. My dear friend Julia, leaving the silence behind, shared with all of us her experience and the reason why she had burst into tears. When my turn arrived, I was speechless and immediately tried to avoid the subject. How could I explain such a transformative experience in a couple of minutes or even hours? I knew what I had experienced was only the beginning of a transcendental transformation. That session had erased my old perception of romantic relationships, leaving a blank space that had to be filled with a new perception molded by me, not by society, parents, or friends. But what worried me most was that I was still married to and living with Joe, and I had no idea how this detachment would affect our relationship.

The Consequences

We spent the rest of the afternoon chatting at home. At dusk, my aunt invited us to dinner. Joe joined us at the restaurant after work. I felt so strange seeing him again after what happened that afternoon. However, in that crowded Miami restaurant, while many conversations intertwined around us, I noticed that the knot that had once tied me to him was undone. I knew this broken link was not related to my love for him, for I love him with detachment, and I could still feel the affection was there, intact, still beating within me. I was detached from what he represented in my life, from all the mundane labels and fears that kept us together. The experience was bizarre. Less than eight hours had passed since we were having breakfast together, absorbed in the quotidian, handing over toasts, tea, and confitures. In those minutes, the cord that was now gone was there, tying me to him, making him part of my family and firmly holding us together.

By the end of the dinner, we were all exhausted, so we said our goodbyes. Joe and I returned home, exchanging a few words on the way. When I opened the door to the apartment, a deep feeling of sadness invaded me. I was so confused. I did not know if that would continue being our home, or if we would still be a family after what happened that afternoon. Suddenly I felt the typical lump in my throat, announcing that tears were about to come. I did my best to suppress the sobs that wildly wanted to take hold of me. I needed to get away so I could let my tears and my sobs come out. I told Joe that I was going to walk Rocco— the most recent member of our family, a puppy that we had rescued in Costa Rica. I leashed Rocco, closed the door of the apartment, and I let everything out. I was in such a state that I had to take the stairs. Only when I left the building was I able to breathe in again.

It was one of those sticky August nights in South Beach, where the humid breeze brings with it the smell of the ocean, reminding you that you are only a few blocks away from the beach. Walking towards the sea, I noticed the streets crowded with people. Just a couple of years ago, this small residential area within South Beach was a secret among locals. Now it was discovered and full of tourists despite the fact that it was low season in Miami. What was once my slice of paradise now was so alive and hectic that it was impossible for me to walk peacefully and unnoticed towards the beach. To be honest, the people who walked euphorically smiling and talking didn't match with my tears.

I tried to walk mainly through residential streets, avoiding contact with lost tourists. In a desperate attempt to save my marriage, I analyzed what had happened during the breathing experience. I could feel my detachment from believing that one of the main objectives in life was to marry or to find a Prince Charming with whom to live for the rest of the days. Finding someone to share life with was simply an experience like any other, never the main goal in life, as I always believed. I also realized that while a healthy relationship required some compromises, great sacrifices only appeared when we were forcing the situation. In my case, it was the fear of being alone that made me sacrifice that much. Thankfully, that fear was washed away along with many of my ties. It was that absence of fear that made me reluctant to continue making sacrifices. The beauty of relationships revolve around the words "effortless" and "flow," and ours was pretty far from those terms; in fact, I was pretty sure that my marriage to Joe would never survive without colossal sacrifices.

For the first time, I was left doing all the dirty work. In all my previous detachment processes, everything was straightened out without any effort on my part. In this one, I had to face the consequences and decide if I would continue with actions that supported the detachment or ignore what I experienced that day. All those reasonings were summed up in a simple decision that would require an emptied mind and closed eyes; this was something that needed to be felt and not analyzed. So I disconnected my mind and continued walking aimlessly in a meditative state. Only when I was totally exhausted did I find the courage to look for the crucial answer in the place occupied by my heart. Once I found the answer, I asked myself the question for the last time: Do you want to continue being married to Joe?

My answer was a sincere and straightforward, "No." Although I loved Joe as I had never loved anyone, I had reached a crossroads in my life where I felt I needed to put myself first. Whenever I made a sacrifice during our relationship, I gave away a part of me, with no fight, no resistance. I couldn't continue giving myself away. All of those sacrifices were simply proof of a conflict within me, and after what I had experienced that afternoon, I couldn't look away. I needed time to process everything and clarify my understanding regarding romantic relationships, and being involved in one was not going to help. The simple no that I had given as an answer allowed me to understand that there was nothing I could do to stay with Joe, so I turned around and returned home.

A Matter of Social Conditioning

During the following days, I gave myself the time needed to assimilate what had happened. Joe worked until late, so most of the time, when he got home, I was ready to go to bed. During my ponderings, I was able to track the beginning of this process to those days when I felt discouraged. I remember that I also noticed my sacrifices in the marriage back then, but I had pushed them aside, thinking they were not related to this self-study. It was only in Costa Rica when, after the end of my dark night, I was able to confirm that something in my marriage was definitely not right. There, I could not only see my sacrifices, but I could also see Joe's. The substantial renunciations on both sides were cracks in our relationship that sooner or later would make it all fall apart. I recognize that if this path hadn't allowed me to see my attachments, we could have stayed in together for many, many years until the stillness of the cracks couldn't hold us together any longer.

It was only after my detachment episode that I was able to entirely disconnect from my mundane perceptions regarding relationships. Then, it became evident to me how the social conditioning I had been subjected to since childhood created the foundation upon which I had built my romantic life. As a result, finding someone to spend the rest of my life with had become one of my main goals in life, since I blindly believed in the equations:

LOVE = HAPPINESS

MONEY = HAPPINESS

LOVE + MONEY = HAPPINESS^2

Sadly, the love I was conditioned to look for was not the love within. On the contrary, it was the love of others that I learned to madly crave. As a result, all the affection and approval I received from others was all the affection and approval I had for myself. It wasn't until that September day when my niece was born, and I felt the boundless and overflowing love living within me, that I discovered that relationships do not appear in our lives to provide us with love. That day it became evident that nobody could give a love as infinite and pure as the one that already lives within all of us.

Unfortunately, I was not only looking for affection in my relationships, I also expected to receive company, security, and social acceptance, among many other things. So even though I loved Joe with detachment and had no need to be loved by him, I was still a slave to the mundane by all of those other ties that tainted our union.

I never realized that Joe and I were both attached to the idea of a forever together until the breathing experience. We had chosen to celebrate a humanistic wedding believing that we couldn't care less about the rules of society, but the reality was that we never escaped from replicating what society had instilled in us: that terrible habit of holding on to things, ideas, and people. We wanted our relationship to last till death do us part. So, we pursued that crazy idea where everything must stay the same: static, motionless, and frozen in time in order for us to be happy and feel safe. Why was it so difficult for us to see that there is nothing, absolutely nothing static in the Universe? Why was it so difficult for us to accept that everything in the Universe was created to be in continuous motion?

Thus, we ended up trying to achieve this perfect image of a love frozen in time, of growing old together, and we focused so much on it that we ultimately disconnected ourselves from the present. We sacrificed our todays to build an aging together that we may never attain. How long did we think we could bear our unhappiness before we exploded? How did we convince ourselves that sacrificing essential aspects of our lives and ourselves for a relationship was reasonable?

When all of my foundations started to shake and all of this social conditioning was challenged by the divine knowledge within me, my attachment was finally exposed. Although I must admit that I tried for a few days to ignore what I saw, it was useless, because soon enough, I was violently shaken by an unsolicited detachment. And you might think that by having a wealth of divine knowledge within me, I would have a clearer idea of what to do next, but the reality was that no such clues were given to me. On the contrary, all my core beliefs were ripped out, leaving an empty space that haunted me for weeks. All I could do was to commit to give myself all the time needed to process it all. I didn't want my brain to elaborate on the responses I didn't have. I wanted to leave my mind as far away as possible from that empty space within me. It had to be my being who filled in those gaps and answered all of my questions. I was not in a hurry; on the contrary, I had the rest of my life for this beautiful task.

The End

Days later, when I explained to Joe how I felt, we were both immediately caught up in the mundane acts that precede any separation: recriminations about "You did this and that" and "What would happen if you change this and I change that?" However, our hearts knew that what was happening was more significant and more profound than that worldly camouflage.

Joe confirmed my suspicions, sharing with me that he was so committed to making it work and so sure that he wanted us to spend the rest of our lives together, that like me, he found himself forcing everything since the beginning. So, he sacrificed things that were very important to him during these two years for the sake of the marriage.

It took us a few days to admit it and make peace with the fact that we were the only ones responsible for taking that relationship so far with so much sacrifice on both sides. A week later, we separated, and it was the most civilized breakup I've ever had. I can't deny that I still love him and always will. I lived with him the two most beautiful and magical years of my life.

What worried me the most after the separation was Troy's reaction. The same day Joe and I decided to go on different paths, I picked Troy up from school and told him I wanted to have a serious conversation with him as soon as we got to the apartment. I remember once we got there, he took the books out of his backpack and sat at the table to begin his homework. I have to confess I was a little nervous since I had no idea how he would react. Then I sat next to him and asked for his attention. I was very frank with him. I told him how I felt and the reasons why we had separated. As soon as I finished, he just looked up to me and said, "I knew it!" He reminded me of that time in Costa Rica, when he saw us arguing and asked, "Are you going to get divorced?" I always tend to forget how children have this sixth sense more awakened than ours. After reminding me that he already suspected it, he looked me in the eyes and made me promise that we would continue surfing. Once I nodded, he smiled and continued with his homework. I was extremely puzzled by his composure, but moments like those reminded me of his connection and detachment from everything, a duality that I have always longed for.

Only when the separation was a fact did I feel the immense relief I usually felt during all the detachment processes I experienced along this path. However, what made this separation an extraordinary and unique process was that it finally emancipated my being, making it overflow with dazzling and intoxicating freedom. This new freedom kept me vibrating in a state of bliss for more than two months, and during each one of those days, I felt as if at any moment my feet would come off the ground allowing my body to float away slowly, as most of the knots that once tied me to this world were finally gone.

If you ask me if I still believe in relationships that can last "till death do us part," the answer is yes, I do think they exist. What I do not believe in is the idea that life's main goal consists of looking for a person to be by our side or being attached to the notion that our life is only going to be complete when we find that person. My life will always be whole, and I am aware that finding a man with whom to share the rest of my days is an experience that I may or may not be able to live in this life.

However, today all of that has lost importance. The romantic aspect of my life has significantly shrunk as I have recognized the importance of many other areas. When I was previously tortured by love and money, I now felt surrounded by endless treasures—such as surfing, writing, reading, traveling, new adventures, and new friends—that infused my life with sublime magic and fascinating novelty. I stopped looking for more of the same and used the newfound freedom to find more of those little treasures and moments that infuse my life with exquisite freshness.

The freedom I enjoyed from this detachment invited me to exist as that divine energy that is all around and within us, that which is in constant motion and flows like the rest of the Universe. As that energy, I just wanted to follow my essence, the one that invited me to experience everything without clinging to anything, the one that led me to expose myself to new ideas, situations, and people. This new way in which I started to see life, where experiences are the Holy Grail, helped me to clarify a misconception under which I lived my entire life. Finally, I could comprehend that the voice that had always instigated me to want more of life was actually my self being led by my essence. The issue was that "the more of life" never implied more love, more money, more sex, more things; it simply meant more experiences, as it is only from experiences that our being feeds from.

After this last transcendental discovery, I was stricken by the realization that the book never felt complete because it never wanted to end like a fairy tale, where its characters lived happily ever after. I imagine the book was always waiting for this section... when armed with courage, I finally listened to my being. The section where I understood that I am not what I was led to believe. The part of the book where experiencing only an iota of absolute freedom. I was able to connect with the divine energy to finally understand that there is no other aim in life than simply experiencing and feeling with all of our beings every moment of our existence.

THE END

THE TIME HAS COME to let go of your hand and part on different paths, saying goodbye to that invisible and fleeting force that made our stories collide, but before I would love to share with you the wish that materialized this book...the one in which I longed for these pages to sparkle in others the same magic that *Autobiography of a Yogi* scattered in mine. So, when your time is right, all that magic germinates within you, attracting your highest path.

AFTERWORD

How Meditation Works

When I first started meditating, I was a practical person who saw meditation as a methodical exercise that may or may not solve all my problems, and, frankly, I didn't mind trying it. I never considered the practice as a spiritual one, since I firmly believed the mysticism some found in it depended solely on the practitioner.

Today, it is evident to me that I was just lying to myself. Otherwise, how could anyone think there is nothing mystical, magical, or spiritual in a technique in which you close your eyes, waiting for your life to change?

In my life prior to meditation, I had always secretly sheltered a kindled hope of a non-palpable world, even though my rational mind had constantly rejected the realness of the imperceptible. Luckily, it is within this aspect that meditation begins to work its magic.

As I progressed through the ancient practice, I couldn't ignore its spiritual side. Sooner rather than later, I was able to perceive and connect with the Divine, with that supreme power that lives within and around us. I remember one day, full of curiosity, I asked myself: who is connecting with the Divine? Is it my being? My mind? Or my body? Although, the answer was: all three! It was only my mind that had the ability to be aware of that connection. I had finally found the link through which I could connect my mind with the intangible spiritual world I always secretly hope existed.

With the delightful naïveté of a new pupil, I named this new path "my journey towards enlightenment," unaware that I was being guided towards what man has sought through the centuries: the ability to perceive and realize the Divinity and the Supreme Power.

I consider the content of this Afterword to be the most significant and valuable contribution of my entire life. Its importance sets it apart from the rest of the narrative, leaving it, however, as the axis on which all the experiences locked in the rest of the book smoothly swivel around.

To facilitate the understanding of such a complicated subject, I will initially share a summary of the internal processes that make our transformation possible. According to my experience, during the first process activated through meditation, our Being works toward regaining its sovereignty over our thinking faculty. Only in those instances when our Being reigns is it possible to initiate two other processes, one in which we begin to perceive small fragments of the Supreme Power within us and another in which we absorb part of the Divine Knowledge that Supreme Power is made of. Once that knowledge is absorbed and stored in our mind in its purest form, we must go through a process of realization in which it is put into practice in our day-to-day life to become ours and be ultimately stored in our consciousness. It should be noted that the more we meditate and the more we connect with our Being, the more we manage to experience the divine and accumulate the knowledge necessary to raise our consciousness.

In the following pages, I share how these processes started within me:

Recovering Our Sovereign Over Our Thinking Faculty

I remember that in those first days when I sat down to meditate, all I could perceive was the enormous effort I made trying not to think. The idea that something else was happening within me while I meditated never crossed my mind. I was trying so hard that when the minutes passed and my meditations ended, I was left feeling like a total loser because I couldn't manage to keep my mind blank for more than a second. I was convinced by then that the time I was in the land of "no thoughts" was the only thing that mattered. The reality is that every second of the entire practice is of utmost importance, as during that time, a delicate battle is waged within our minds to gain back control over our thinking faculty.

Thinking has obviously taken over our minds. Most of us find ourselves thinking the majority of our waking hours, absolutely unaware that this faculty is simply a survival tool meant to be used on certain occasions to find solutions to problems. The mind was not created to remain constantly active, thus eliminating those quiet instances where our being gets to prevail over our minds and bodies.

Only when we stop thinking, and our mind is blank, are we awarded precious moments of conscious existence. During those seconds, each one of the faculties of our mind experience what it is to be like those trees that dance with the wind, like that placid sea that lets us see our reflection or like those clouds that dance through the skies.

The more I meditated, the more I began to feel the thinking faculty like a muscle that you want to get fit, so you develop a workout routine and start doing the exercises to be rewarded in time with the results you wanted. For me, meditation was the workout routine that retrained my thinking faculty to withdraw, to stop taking over, so my being could reign, but still being present and alert when needed.

One day, after many, many practices, there was no more forcing and no more struggle. Meditation became like a dance you know by heart, and by which I was delightfully carried away. I didn't stop thinking 100 percent of the time, but I managed to stop thinking when I wanted to for longer and longer periods.

Perceiving the Divine

Perception is the faculty of the mind in charge of organizing, identifying, and interpreting the information received through our senses.

Usually, the first few times that we meditate, there is no perception, because our let's call it "sixth sense" is still dormant. However, with daily practice, the sixth sense awakens, giving us the most precious gifts that meditation can grant: the ability to perceive the Higher Self, not only with our sixth sense but also with our bodies and with our minds—when we get to feel tingling sensations, bliss, floating in nothingness, or even hearing the divine sound of Om.

Some practitioners take longer to perceive the supreme power despite making meditation a daily practice; this does not mean that they cannot experience it or are not fit for it. We all are. Some people might have to fight many more battles with their minds in order for their sixth sense to come to life. The most common struggles we face during this process include: not trusting in the process, not practicing honestly, doing it only to cross it off our list, not surrendering to accept what is given to us, and trying to control the process through having expectations that we want to to be met. Each of the battles to be fought varies depending on the individual and the lessons they must learn to advance on the path; all you need is a sincere desire for your union with the supreme power, the one that has all the answers.

Divine insights came to me quickly after just a few weeks of practicing my regular meditations. I suppose that my prompt exposure to this mystical world resulted from my unexpectant approach. In those days, I never anticipated sublime experiences from this practice, much less such sudden cues that I was on the right path.

At first, my perceptions were based simply on feeling that I existed, but little by little, they evolved, granting me episodes of absolute happiness, connection to the universe, and pure love. Although all my perceptions were only iotas of the supreme power, for me, they meant everything. For the first time in my life, I was able to feel with my body and interpret with my mind the God that I had read in books or heard from the lips of religious people... there were no longer doubts because the divinity was already palpable.

At this point, I find it crucial to warn practitioners not to waste their time sitting down to meditate, expecting to receive these divine perceptions. The path traveled through meditation is not created by us; it is instead tailored to us. We cannot dictate or manipulate what is going to happen or what we are going to learn from our meditations. We must totally surrender and trust the Universe will guide us at its own perfect pace... never ours. Not trying to control and not anticipating these perceptions while keeping an honest desire for our union with the Divine is the only way to surrender and to show confidence in the process.

My Perception of Reality

In the following lines, I will share my current perception of reality with you, which is how I see the entire universe today. This is only my perception of reality; I am not asserting that it is yours, much less that it is the absolute truth. There are more than seven billion people living on this planet, so there are more than seven billion perceptions of reality; mine is simply one of those.

All the transcendental experiences that I have lived through these two years have brought me into contact one way or another with a Divine Energy. Over time I managed to understand that this energy contains the absolute knowledge and power, as God might have. According to what I have been able to perceive, this divinity does not reveal itself as gas, water, or solid. Yet, it is these three elements at the same time, for it is everything, existing thus before anything else, even before the creation of the universe.

As the essence of energy is movement and movement translates into change and evolution, this energy has always been in constant change, evolving into different forms: gas, water, solid, fire, stars, planets, plants, animals, human beings, and everything else in the universe. Therefore, everything that exists in it is just different versions of that same Divine Energy, and each one of those versions contains the same absolute power and knowledge. They all have the same essence. They all are evolving, moving forward, working together, interconnected and following the same flow, because even though they seem different, they are actually all the same.

The only plan of this Divine Energy is to exist, and having movement as its essence is what gives it the opportunity to exist in all forms possible, from being that Saturn that seems to float in space, that grass that we step on in the park, or even as that child who lives in the worst circumstances.

In the wonderful journey of this Divine Energy, there is no good or bad evolution. For this energy, there is nothing wrong with being that child who lives in the worst conditions imaginable, that grass constantly stepped on, because the only thing who aspires to this Divine Energy is Being, the experience to exist in all possible forms.

Acquiring Divine Knowledge

What I find incredibly fascinating about meditation is its irony, because we end up frustrated after our first sessions by not being able to keep our minds blank for more than a second. But it is in that shy second when most of the magic of meditation occurs. You don't need to wait to have several minutes of a quiet mind for meditation to work, as everything within us happens at the speed of light. All it takes is a few seconds of our brain being suspended into nothingness for our true nature—which is Divine Energy—to regain its sovereignty, allowing us to absorb bits of the Divine Knowledge contained in it.

Many people consider the absorption of this Divine Knowledge as the most important aspect of meditation. Thus, it is the one that allows us to advance to higher consciousness. Although you might think that after meditating and accumulating all this Divine Knowledge there should be no more effort on our part, the reality is entirely different, because it is exactly here when we begin the most challenging part of our journey through meditation. Having iotas of the Divine Knowledge navigating within our mind does not make us elevated or enlightened beings. We need the necessary tools to reach magical moments of realization, where that raw Divine Knowledge is deciphered, understood, and assimilated by our mind until it becomes part of our knowledge and ready to be stored in our consciousness.

Magical Moments of Realization

When I first thought about following a higher consciousness path, I knew that many changes needed to take place within me for that to happen. Over time, I understood that an inward change couldn't occur without a shift in our perception. I eventually started to call those episodes "magical moments of realization" because somehow, almost inexplicably, something happens within us that helps us decipher that raw Divine Knowledge that we have been acquiring through meditation, making it our own.

The process by which those magical moments of realization can materialize begins when the Divine Knowledge that we have acquired thanks to our meditations challenges the mundane knowledge we have developed throughout our lives. For this to happen, we need to experience situations where our intellect needs to use our knowledge to establish judgments and make decisions.

My contact with these magical moments of realization started early on my journey. I was so committed to the practice that after only a week, the Divine Knowledge absorbed during my meditations began to increase significantly. By then, various situations I was going through in my life started to instigate a battle between my mundane and my recently acquired Divine Knowledge. These wars could last days, weeks, or months and only ended with those magical moments of realization.

At first, amid my ignorance, I saw these processes—which I began to call self-studies—as a series of wicked milestones on my way to enlightenment. Most of them tormented me enormously and caused terrible pain. Although you might think that I would adapt and suffer less every time a new process started, this never happened. I suffered through each self-study as if it had been the first.

Much of the Divine Knowledge I absorbed was so radical and profound that it crumbled many of the layers that covered my being. The more layers fell, the more my intellect became familiar with the being that dwells within me.

Sometimes these magical moments of realization can appear in our lives even before the divine perceptions. Nonetheless, the anguish emerging during this process contributes to the deviation of many practitioners from this journey. I have heard an endless number of practitioners quitting meditation and blaming it on sudden chaos and bumps appearing in their life. Some of them were able to sense how meditation attracted that turmoil into their lives, while others simply believed it was bad timing. Certainly, it is much easier to quit, avoiding the turmoil altogether. Still, the understanding and growth that comes from these processes is what generates a transcendental change in our lives.

Raising Our Consciousness

The result of each magic moment of realization I had experienced was summed up in a Divine Knowledge that is now part of me abiding in my consciousness. As more moments of realization occurred, and more Divine Knowledge was assimilated, my consciousness began rising higher and higher. It was as if each particle of Divine Knowledge I got to decipher was a piece of a puzzle, and as they appeared, sections became complete, revealing an even higher knowledge. I remember that on several occasions, I tried to find the answers to some of my questions in that puzzle within my consciousness, and in some of those semi-complete sections, I found hints to my answers.

This higher consciousness I am still getting acquainted with is simply the fruit of all the seeds many people have sown throughout the centuries. Thanks to this awareness, some of us are beginning to see another truth, and another world not governed by our body or by our minds. Instead, we see a realm reigned by our beings by this invisible Divine Energy that is everything. And I can't help being elated by the awe-inspiring world our next generations will get to call home once we unite and unleash all the power of our minds, bodies, and beings. Even when I see this new way of existence is hundreds of years ahead, I still find it deeply inspiring to be part of that engine that now propels that change, that evolution.

ACKNOWLEDGMENTS

It has been incredible how the writing of these pages has brought into my life people of unquestionable talent and immense devotion to what they do. There have been endless manuscripts, but in the final result, you can see the shimmering essence of each one of those who have helped me in this beautiful endeavor, and I cannot be more than infinitely grateful for each one of them: Nury Rincón, Courtney Watson, Christine LePorte, Jennifer Pope, Jessica Black, Jackie Cangro, and Christy Risco.

I wanted to also express my gratitude to those wonderful friends that many of us have, those who with just a hug, a glance, or simply putting their hand over ours, instantly connect us with our Highest Self, and with all that love that we carry inward, for me those friends are: Jenny García, Aysun Batum, Perla Herrera, and Julia Fraga. They are also the ones who have contributed with their valuable time reading the manuscript in its different stages, and donating invaluable feedback.

The most special thanks to my sister Fernanda, who has been the engine that has driven me to continue every time I secretly wanted to give up, who smiled each one of the thousands of times I said the book was finished, and who has designed the beautiful book cover.

Thanks to Joe and my son, Troy, two beings of immense light who accompanied me throughout this journey and who, with just their presence, inspired me to reach heights I had never dreamed of.

Finally, the dearest of thanks to my parents who had guided and accompanied me through this delightful adventure called life.

Made in the USA
Monee, IL
25 November 2020

49634332R00125